Disclaimer

This book is a work of non-fiction and reflects the personal experiences, views, and interpretations of the author. While every effort has been made to ensure the accuracy of the information, some names, characters, and identifying details have been changed to protect the privacy of individuals. While certain characters and events in this book are based on real-life experiences and people, the author has altered identifying information to preserve anonymity. Any resemblance to actual persons, living or dead, may be intentional but does not reflect the complete identities of those individuals.

This book contains discussions about cryptocurrency and offers readers tokens at the end of each chapter for engagement purposes. These tokens are provided for educational and interactive purposes only and do not represent any form of financial investment, security, or currency. The tokens offered are not intended to have any monetary value, and the author and publisher make no guarantees regarding their future value or usability.

The information provided in this book regarding cryptocurrency, blockchain technology, or any other financial topics is for informational purposes only and does not constitute financial, legal, or investment advice. Readers are encouraged to conduct their own research and consult with a qualified financial advisor before making any financial decisions, including the purchase or use of cryptocurrencies.

The author, publisher, and any associated entities disclaim all liability for any loss or damage incurred as a result of the use, purchase, or reliance on the cryptocurrency or tokens mentioned in this book. By accepting and using the tokens offered in this book, the reader acknowledges that they do so at their own risk and that neither the author nor the publisher is liable for any financial or legal consequences that may arise.

HOW I MET GOD & GOT INTO CRYPTO

Vol-1

ADHITYA IYER

BASED ON A TRUE STORY

HOW I MET GOD & GOT INTO CRYPTO

Vol-1

ILLUSTRATIONS
LEKHA D

ISBN
Paperback 979-8-89498-369-1
Hardcase 979-8-89556-624-4

Dedicated to

Amma - Visalakshi Sundar Iyer (aka Usha)

&

To All the Mothers in the World…

Contents

Acknowledgement

With deepest gratitude and immense Love, I would love to thank and acknowledge those mentioned below (and those I haven't or missed) for making this book possible -

I don't fully understand why but the Acknowledgement section is one of my most cherished parts of writing a book. The sheer joy of going through an adventurous journey, being able to share it, and at the end being able to thank all those wonderful passengers who made the journey possible! As "Bali Influncer"ish as it may sound, gratitude does invoke something beautiful within ourselves! So here we go - While I could do an entire book on just this section, I am mentioning here only those who have directly been involved in making this story and its telling possible -

Amma, Appa, my Grandparents and entire ancestry. Genes play such a crucial role in what we do and seldom receive the acknowledgement they deserve. I would like to thank my entire Genetic lineage from the bottom of my heart because it made a lot of my life easy, including writing this book, without much effort on my side.

Devi Amma for her unconditional love.

Suresh *Appa* for always having my back.

My sister Soumya - although not directly involved with this book much but mentioning her in hope that she can wave off the money I owe her.

Lekha who with her child-like unflinching love and support has enriched the book and every other aspect of the project in ways I did not imagine. Her illustrations add much more flavor to the experience of this book.

The generously co-operative Katherine(Katia Ram) whose illustrations at the start of every chapter have enhanced the book in beautiful ways you shall see for yourself.

Darshan Ashar, a childhood accomplice(and victim) in and of my adventures. His involvement in this book too hasn't been much but mentioning him so as to continue receiving 15% Apple Employee Discount on all my Apple purchases.

Tanush Parihar, Prashant Ghabak(including his wife Aditi, and Baby Meera) - for donning multiple roles - friends, family, graceful hosts, and for this book, also as Beta Readers.

Harish Balani and his family whose warm company made Doha, where important chunks of this book were written, very homely for me and also for his contribution as a Beta Reader(I think he completed reading the book in a go on his flight from India to Qatar).

Cafe Einstein in Bern, Switzerland where important chunks of the book have been written.

The entire global Aviation Industry and Airport Staff who work tirelessly through days and nights to ensure that *Musafirs* like me can have the sort of experiences we crave for. I think airline travel is no less than a miracle! To be able to travel from one end of the world to another, in a matter of a few hours, in a comfortable seat, while being served delicious food & beverage, with a screen to pick stuff to watch from? Uff!

Pratham Booth, the kind friend from college who lent me his laptop on which I wrote my first book. Believe it or not, I somehow missed mentioning him totally in the acknowledgement section there. Making up for it by thanking him profusely for his generosity.

All my Beta Readers - I ran an extensive Beta Readership program for over a year before publishing this book - obsessively seeking feedback - and choosing people from the most unlikely places and seeking their kind participation. A few special mentions -

Sukanya Yadav for being a perennial cheerleader and support throughout the project and for having the most layered, intuitive and nuanced understanding and feedback on everything being done with the book - both by words & beyond.

Aditi Gupta, who wrote me an unassuming email after reading my first book while I was conducting my Beta Readership program for this one. I quickly(and thankfully) pulled her into the program for this book and she is now an integral and cherished part of my core team!

Sravani Akuthota - whose candid, unrestrained and sharp insights & feedback helped me add more context and perspective to the book.

Ankita Jha for taking the time and patiently reading the chapters - almost overnight - on my request - and being so sharp and curious with her feedback.

Sahaj Kedia, whose has contributed to the project not only as a Beta reader but whose development efforts have led to the creation of the website that you shall get to experience in course of reading this book.

Rahul Nagaraj & Seema Tharani from Team Agna - who took precious time off their schedule to read and give such pointed feedback at a crucial junction of the book.

Narangidevi Joshi (Pranchal) for her back to back reading & intuitive feedback.

Vinayak Singla, Ayaan Khan, Amar Naik, Ekta Mourya, Khushi Sharma, Phanindra, Pranav Rajgopal, Swe Sin Tha - I looked forward to your feedback with great anticipation. Your early support meant a lot to me - a lot more than you can imagine.

Mumbai and my beautiful house there, Bengaluru and its various residences that have hosted me through the course of this book - the only two cities I currently call home and have received so much from.

Coffee Angadi and Fab Hotel at Jayanagar 9th Block.

Foram Tambawala whose friendship knowingly or unknowingly helped me tide through difficult times and for her contribution to the Beta Readership as well.

Prachi Ma'am & Godbole sir from my Engineering college Sardar Patel Institute of Technology whose love and support shaped an important phase of my life.

Satoshi Nakamoto and the entire crypto community.

Varun Nadkarni, Sneha Solanki - two dear friends I would like to make a very special mention of here for reasons that they may not fully understand now but in Volume 2 of the book it will become clear.

My iPhone & Mac - intimate associates and constant companions on which this book was written.

Midjourney, DallE, ChatGPT - Technology is truly one of the greatest blessings for mankind.

Music - one of nature's most beautiful creations and man's greatest discoveries.

Cigarettes - particularly the brand I smoke - Classic Ice Burst - proved to be a great support to me through the journey of writing this book.

Filter Coffee - The Greatest Coffee in the world!

The Sun, Moon, & Wind - Constant companions no matter which part of the world I am in.

Food Delivery and Quick commerce Apps Zomato, Zepto, Swiggy, Talabat that fed my craving and requirements even at the oddest hour. What a time to be living in!

Nakul for playing an important cameo in my advent to Web3.

Shubham, my former Web3 colleague, for really being a nice guy in general and for gifting me a 4 letter sol domain.

Zhen & Leonard for being such a wonderful team of founders and for giving my me first Web3 break.

Arya Vashisht, Rajat Agrawal, Vishesh Gupta for being co-operative roomies!

Rohit Bhangale for gifting me my first Jordans - almost like an early reward for completing the book!

Palash, Abhijit, Arunabh and the entire TVF fam!

Eva, my friend in Bern, Switzerland who led me to an important location in the story.

Publisher NotionPress.

Sanjana who was a catalyst for a pivotal moment in the story and the journey.

You, the Reader…

Lekha's Acknowledgment

"I wanna thank myself for going through this 3 year long project with all the drama in between & surviving it all alive XD " ~ Lekha D

Preface

I started writing this book while I was in India, and a large part of it was conceptualised and written there. Parts of the book have been conceived and/or written during my stays in Paris, Amsterdam, Luxembourg, Qatar, UAE, Singapore, Brussels, and Berlin. However, the words you are reading right now (and certain other sections of the book) are being written (almost totally by chance!) in a rather interesting place - a cafe named after a man who married his own cousin, never saw his first daughter, if he ever went to an Indian school, 5th-grade bullies would call him "Maggi noodles" over his now iconic hairdo, he refused the Presidency of Israel, was spied on by the FBI for decades and on the side, also made some scientific discoveries - I'm of course talking about Albert Einstein. The cafe is called - (take a wild guess) - Cafe Einstein! I mean, I would have hoped they were more imaginative than that? For example, I would perhaps have called it Cafe Spooky Einstein or Cafe Einstainglement (Sounds so German, no?) in reference to his dismissive remark on the remarkable concept of "Quantum Entanglement" in Quantum Physics. I feel one subject that comes closest to life is Quantum Physics. If you truly want to "understand" life, you must "understand" Quantum Physics, but there is a problem - you cannot. Quantum Physics cannot be understood - you must keep trying until someday, you just get it. In Quantum Physics, there is a beautiful concept called Quantum Entanglement which basically suggests that the state of one particle has a direct impact on the state of a totally different particle. Confused? Let me explain using a Bollywood movie.

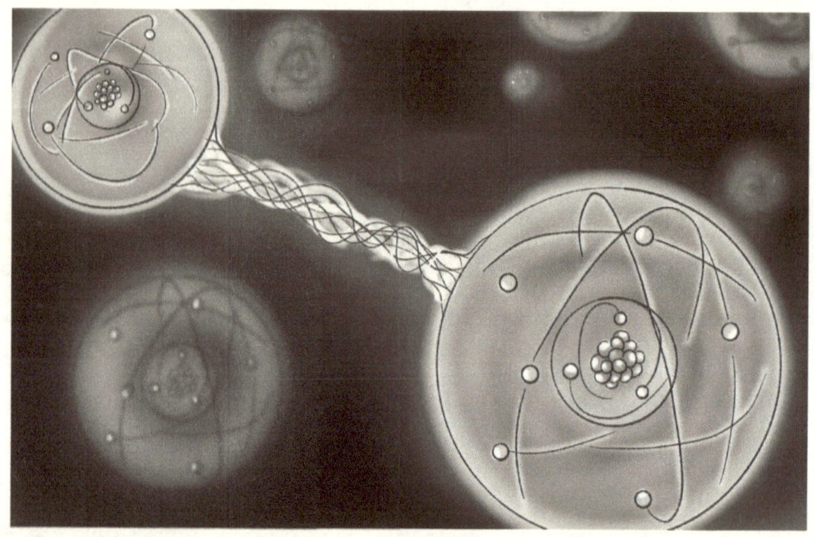

There is a Bollywood classic from the 90s called "Judwaa" (meaning "Twins" in English). The lead star Salman Khan went on to become one of the biggest and most controversial film stars in India, and this movie played a huge role in it. It's also funny how Salman came about doing this movie. The then reigning Bollywood superstar Govinda(fondly known as Chichi) was initially cast for the movie and had even started shooting for it. One night, at roughly 2 am or so, he receives a call from Salman saying, "How many hits will you give *Chichi* Bhaiya? Keep some for us also," and after that call, Govinda handed over the movie to Salman. That's it. It is ridiculous how much impact a perfectly crafted sentence can have on you. Now in the movie Judwaa, a pair of identical twins separated at birth grow up with totally contrasting upbringings. One grows up to become a sophisticated, rich suave man, and the other an uncouth street goon. In the climax, the goon is tragically locked up with his loving and obedient sidekick and unable to fight, while his twin, who had perhaps never even killed a mosquito his entire life, must now confront a menacing villain whom he must defeat in order to save his brother and the rest of his family. What happens next? The twin locked up in jail starts beating up his sacrificial sidekick, and guess what?! - in what is possibly the earliest demonstration of Quantum Entanglement, his twin's body miraculously responds in the exact same manner as his brother, and he ends up beating the villain! Whoever said that one must leave their brains behind to watch a Bollywood movie was clearly wrong. Einstein found this (this as in Quantum Entanglement and not the movie, of course) too ridiculous to be true and called it "spooky action at a distance." Life is so strange, no?

Anyway, coming back to our cafe, as you can see below, they have rather intelligent branding on their cups.

The Cafe is not named Einstein without reason, though. The Cafe is located right below the apartment where Einstein lived with his (first) wife and son, and more significantly, it is where he developed and wrote the "Theory of Relativity" that, as we now know, has changed the course of modern-day physics and our understanding of the cosmos. Not a bad place to write a book on God (and crypto, given Switzerland's reputation as the world's bank!).

Now, why is the book titled 'How I Met God & Got into Crypto?' Am I being clickbaity? No! I am not. This book will indeed talk about what the title promises - and much more. Now, I know the title sounds ridiculous. If somebody told me this 10 years ago, I would have laughed in disbelief, too. In fact, as I rewrite this preface, I still laugh. My views on religion and God are best reflected in this Quora answer I wrote many years ago:

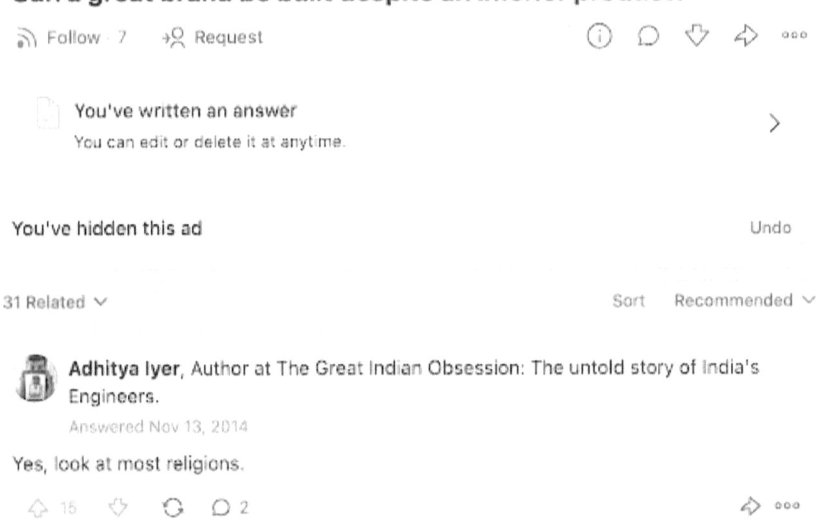

I must now address a standard question and quickly get it out of the way: "Why should you read this book?"

This book, at its core, is about how I found my purpose in life - which involves God & Crypto. Initially, I thought or was rather made to believe that purpose is something we make up to make our life more meaningful and that life itself has no purpose. That's when I came to know about a beautiful & forgotten Indian life principle which I believe is long due for revival. Before I get to the concept, let's discuss a rather cute idea that has gained immense popularity in the world these days - Ikigai. For those unaware, Ikigai, a Japanese concept of life, literally translates to "reason for being" and recommends a sort of formula for living a life of purpose. The guideline it offers is to find one's purpose by narrowing down on that one thing that you love (your passion), the world needs (your mission), you are good at (your vocation), and you can get paid for (your profession). Simple, right? Exactly! This is exactly the problem with Ikigai - it is way too simple to be practical for something much more nuanced and enormous, such as life. Of course, it's a no-brainer - everybody would love to do something they love, that others need, that they are good at, and then also make money from it! But the problem with it is twofold -

1. It relies heavily on what you do on the outside, in terms of your worldly activity, without any consideration for how you feel within yourself.

2. The bigger problem is this: let's say you end up finding your Ikigai. Now, that your passion is also your means of income, for how long would you continue to remain passionate about it? If your passion now has the added pressure of paying your bills, would you be able to do it as passionately and freely?

3.   It is highly impractical. Just by sheer probability and market economics, there are only so many skill sets in the world that would fit into these buckets, and thereby, only a few people could, at least on paper, lead a purposeful life. What about the others? This means Ikigai is not Truth - it is only an idea or a philosophy. What do I mean by that? If something has to be Truth, it has to be applicable to everyone and everything at all times - A universal law - like a rule embedded by the creator as part of the creation. Anyone can come up with any Idea or philosophy but the Truth only comes from the creator and can only be discovered or realized.

What's the solution, then? This is where this book comes into the picture. This book arises from my unflinching pursuit of Truth. For this coming paragraph, let's act all cool and fancy and deep and stuff, okay, then get back to business.

In the Indian context, what one does for a living - known as *artha* - is separate from one's purpose, and this brings us to the core theme of our book, - *Swadharma* - loosely put - the sheer purpose of your existence. What is *Swadharma* exactly? You know, I get asked often how my life has changed since my "spiritual journey" or, as I prefer calling it - "Cosmic Bigg Brother" (or Bigg Boss, depending on which part of the world you live in) - as in you know, living in monasteries, travelling to mystical places, meeting so many "Gurus" and "spiritually evolved" beings and yogis and monks, and all the spiritual practices, yoga, meditation etc - and my answer always baffles people - the bewilderment in their face is too conspicuous to miss - always - I simply tell them that "I am now a better actor." What is this even supposed to mean? The most significant discovery of my life that shook the foundations of my existence is the realisation that who I am is different from the role I play (which I assumed to be myself all my life until that moment!). Every great act involves 3 core aspects - knowing who you are, knowing what your role is, and knowing when to get off your role. Unfortunately, most people don't live with this sense of distinction between who they are and what their role is and end up suffering their role (and, in extreme cases, killing themselves like Heath Ledger). Your *Swadharma* is essentially the unique role you and only you are here to play and are expected to play with perfection. Knowing your *Swadharma* is only one part of the job; the other and equally important part is how you perform your *Swadharama* - like an act and nothing more or less - without getting entangled and carried away with it - and that is why knowing who you are and being in touch with yourself is so crucial. Now, the grand question is how do we know who we are, how do we stay in touch with it, and how do we know what our role in this cosmic drama is? That's why this book, silly! I open my life up to you, for you. We're all eventually passengers in this grand journey - adventurers chartering unknown territories. Here I am, just doing my bit for my fellow travellers, making it a little easier for them, just as those before me have made it easier for me! This entire book is essentially about how I discovered this lost principle, what it is, and how I arrived at my purpose - my *Swadharma* - which involves God & Crypto - 2 of the most crucial and misunderstood subjects of our time.

BE IT LISTENING TO YOUR GRANDMA OR BEING HOOKED TO INSTAGRAM REELS, STORIES HAVE BEEN HUMAN'S OLDEST DRUG !

I did this interesting exercise with my friends while writing this book. I reached out to some of them to describe me in a few lines. There was one that particularly caught my attention, and to date, I don't know why this friend said what he did, but there was something striking about it. There are times in my life when I have observed that while words may be coming out from a particular person, it is not them who is speaking. There is a strange and inexplicable wisdom flowing through them, via them, from a rather strange source. This was one of those moments. He said, "You are the guinea pig that has to go through experiences that others can learn from." There! Quantum Entanglement! I feel my life's story could have an impact on yours in so many ways!

You can count me as that one geeky friend in your circle who doesn't shy away from going deep into the rabbit hole of a subject so that you don't necessarily have to. Imagine when the internet came out in the '90s, or bitcoin in the early 2012, or AI in 2023 - you keep hearing about these fancy things but just don't know where to start, so you reach out to this geeky friend of yours who gives you the perfect orientation so that you can then go on and explore the rest by yourself. This is that kind of book. I love going into rabbit holes and this book is about me entering the rabbit holes of God & Crypto and the truth I discovered about them.

The book is essentially a two-volume adventure . An eternal conflict of Man vs God, Material vs Spiritual. Volume 1 is essentially about Man - me, my journey, and my early exploits in the material world and how it unexpectedly led me to the doorstep of a strange new mystical world, which we will look at more deeply in Volume 2 which is less about me. It's about my stay in the monastery, my encounter with strange beings, places - It's about God, Spirituality, Crypto, & the Cosmos. Volume 2 is an audacious and unprecedented endeavour. Most spiritual books in the past have always been mostly about how the writer, usually a flawless person, is such a great spiritual figure and should you want to become like them, you should do what they did too. Such books do a great disservice to the reader - apart from a sense of lopsided worship and admiration towards the writer, nothing much comes out of it for the reader. Volume 2 of How I Met God & Got Into Crypto will make you an absolute geek about this world of God & Spirituality; it will acquaint you with the why, how, and what of everything. Now that we have dabbled into both worlds - via my internal conflict, it will also address for once the eternal conflict - the grand climax - what is the ultimate purpose of life, God or Material success? Is this world better or that? Everything you read in Vol 1 and 2 will then come together in a big way.

Volume 1 may appear autobiographical, but it is not an autobiography. I've only mentioned those details from my life that add up later to the core theme of the book! Humans are compulsive consumers of stories. From college gossip to Instagram Reels, today, we consume more stories than we ever did. If author Yuval Noah Harari is to be believed, stories have played an unmissable and crucial role in the evolution of man (and woman, of course). If you put food on the table of a hungry man, he will start praying to a God of your choice, but if you feed him the right story, he will start praying to you. Now, this is essentially a storybook. A real story. It is, in fact, a graphic novel. When I first started writing the book, I had an extremely talented collaborator working on the illustrations. I told her on the first day of her job that there could arise a time in the future when she may want to leave the project, and when that day comes, she should be aware. After working for almost a year and completing 40% of the work, she left along with all her illustrations. In what could be one of the most epic promotions of all-time, Lekha, who was then just a gifted intern, reached out to me after she had a random dream about writing a book and then bumping into me via a YouTube video the following day!. After the first collaborator left, Lekha took over as the chief illustrator almost overnight. The beautiful illustrations you see at the start of the chapter are from the gifted - Katherine(Katia Ram) who I specifically requested to be a part of this journey and experience for you

In order to make it an active experience and not just a story, there are 2 things we've done after every chapter. To give you an OG crypto experience, we've added a QR code after every chapter - one you can scan only after completing each chapter (no cheating, please), which will give you some free in-house $GIC tokens (We've created our cryptocurrency for the book, how cool is that? What we(including you) will be doing with $GIC tokens is cutting edge and in so many ways unprecedented - it involves a fascinating confluence of technology, economics, psychology, pop-culture, and meme culture. Don't miss being a part of this process at any cost! You will know why in the course of reading both volumes!). You can use these $GIC tokens to access exclusive bonus content from the book and much more.

For the other theme of the book, we've given a few blank pages after every chapter, which you can use as a personal diary so that Vol 1 also becomes an introspective journey for you. You can either fill in the diary after every chapter or if you do not feel like interrupting your flow, you can also write the diary after you complete reading the book.

I hope I have satisfactorily addressed why you should be reading this book. Now, "Why am I writing this book?" Well, so that I can disappear. There is a deep desire in me to share my life with you, to talk to you, to gossip with you, and express my deep love for you which I hope you can feel in every word I write even if it sounds a lil harsh sometimes! I first explored social media as a potential medium to do so, but social media just lacks the depth and profundity that a book offers. I want this book to be an extremely intimate affair between you and me. Because when I am writing this book, I am lost in talking to you, and I hope you can be lost in my world, too. This book will relieve me of the burden of having to speak unnecessarily anywhere else because everything I want to say now in some way will be in these 2 volumes. So maybe after publishing these books and, later, actively promoting them for a while, I would love to simply disappear, and I cannot wait for that day.

Lastly, I feel I must end with a word of caution now that you are going to be hanging out with me over the next few days. Since childhood, it has been usual for my friends to fall into truble because of me. Many of my friends have fallen into great trouble not because they did something wrong. In their conduct, they were all angel-like. Their only mistake was that they were friends with me. I was what in India we say a "Gone case." When you hopelessly give up on someone, you call them a "Gone Case." Over the years, I had been scolded and beaten by my teachers so much that I developed a thick skin for it, but once, a teacher came up with an innovative way to embarrass me. My childhood friend and I were sitting for a physics class. It couldn't hold my attention for some time, so I cracked a silly joke, and everyone, including my best friend, laughed. To everyone's surprise, my teacher picked on him and not me and reprimanded him in front of the entire class for something he clearly hadn't done. When my friend protested and insisted that it was me who had made the joke and that she was mistaken, the teacher replied, "Adhitya is a Gone Case, we all know that. There is no point telling him anything. It is your mistake that you sit next to him."

I thought it was a fantastic way of reprimanding someone without telling the person anything. So, just in case reading this book and our friendship gets you into trouble, I told you first! Come, fall in trouble with me 🫣

O Dear Love,

Now that you have come,
Please sit down,
I have been waiting for this moment.
First, let me plant you a kiss,
and now,
Let me tell you a story.

Introduction

On the 17th of August 2016, my TEDx talk on "The Interesting Story of our Educational system" was published. While many across the globe have seen the talk, not many know the story behind it. Late in 2015, I published my first book on the fascinating story of what could well be India's fifth biggest religion - engineering. The book, titled The Great Indian Obsession, went on to become a bestseller.

By the time I published the book, I had also become a habitual drinker. It was mainly because I just enjoyed drinking and partly because the tragic findings from my first book on the broken state of India's education system had left me disillusioned. Pretty much for 3 years of my life, I drank every day - I used to consume the equivalent of at least 3-4 pints of beer a day. The experience of alcohol feels significantly enhanced with nicotine in the bloodstream so I also smoked around 10-15 cigarettes a day. I can say now that I was pretty much drinking and smoking away my life, and just then, a girl decided to read my book.

Like many women around the world, this girl grew up with a negative image of her body that would leave a few scars on her personality. By the time she entered the final year of engineering college, with unwavering discipline and grit, she had chiselled her way into what my *MTV Generation* would call a "Hot and Sexy" college babe. Abnormally temperamental, she was also exceptionally smart and sort of a financial whiz kid. Even with a degree in technology, she later managed to secure a banking job with the world's biggest Investment Bank. You may find it surprising, but in India, engineers are interested in doing everything but engineering, so it is not unusual that they become Consultants, Musicians, Marketing Professionals, Bakers, Writers, and even Doctors and Lawyers!

So, this girl read my book and fell in love with it. More significantly, she also fell in love with the author. I fell in love with her, too, but those days, I was also hopelessly in love with alcohol. There were very few things I cherished more than the sound of gulping a chilled, good glass of beer down my throat, soothing its blessed way down to the belly. Ah! So obviously, I sought its intoxicating company every day.

Now, this girl was the founding Chairperson of a local TEDx chapter. TEDx, as you may know, is a globally renowned platform for people who have accomplished something to exchange ideas and inspire others. She insisted I participate as a speaker in the upcoming edition. I wasn't keen because what better do you expect of a man drowned in the enchanting grip of Beauty and Beer? But women usually always have their way with me, so I eventually conceded. By now, through my years in school and college, I had earned quite a reputation as an orator. A possibly well-meaning middle-aged member of an audience once told me, "You are a dangerous person. People listen to you. You are wasting your time. You must join politics, but Alas! I know my words will fall on deaf ears, for you will only listen to Him." How I laughed!

We know a car cannot run on mere reputation. It needs fuel. So, I am preparing and rehearsing every detail of my talk. The storyline, the content, my clothes, my shoes, I know exactly what I want to wear and where I'd pick it up from. I don't know why, but I had this sudden urge to wear a watch. Because I never bothered to own one, I had to borrow one. I'm reviewing my talk on the phone, and I'm inviting my friends over for rehearsals. I'm having unsettling performance anxiety, so I'm also smoking twice the usual cigarettes. I catch a terrible cold and cough, and with just 2 days to go for my talk, she decides to break up. Those days, I used to be a very emotionally delicate and sensitive person. I didn't even have my presentation in order. As any responsible guy on the cusp of a breakthrough opportunity should, I pulled myself together, worked on my presentation, and continued my rehearsals, right? Wrong. I did none of those. Instead, I chose to drink till 4:00 am. After reaching the venue, to make things exponentially worse, I see her walking around. For some reason, she chooses to ignore the fact that I am a guest speaker at the event and misbehaves with me in front of the other guests. I invite a friend over to help me with the presentation, and even at the last minute's notice, like an angel, she quickly drops by and, just in a few minutes, has my presentation in order. With an awfully broken heart, a presentation that was prepared minutes ago, and totally nervous and dejected, I walk on stage. I don't know what happens to me when I walk on the stage. Something takes over me, words flow, and the talk just happens.

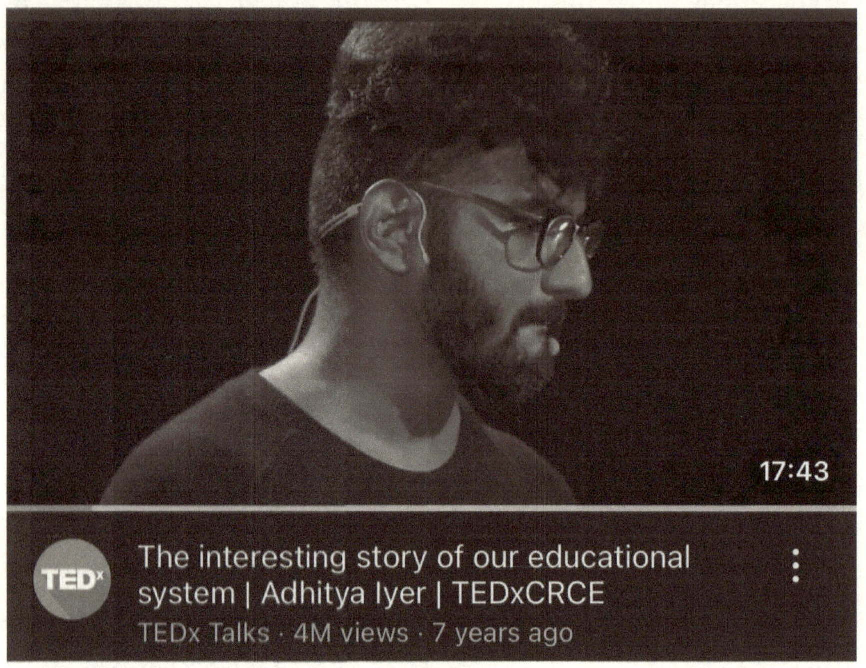

As luck may have it, my TEDx talk went on to become one of the most widely watched talks on education globally, and little did I know what life had in store for me. I was suddenly invited to talks from all over the world with so many questions being thrown at me in anticipation of answers, but there was one problem. I had no answers! I wasn't in the best of shape and had a whole lot of unanswered questions myself, so I found it incredibly ridiculous that I could go around passing any wisdom. By then, my TEDx talk and the book itself became a movement - a movement to transform the global education system. I started receiving multiple emails on my website. My TEDx talk started with thousands of comments, and I set out to take all these enraged people with me to change the education system of the world, but then something totally unexpected happened. I walked into my own death…

Please scan this code to unlock $GIC tokens and
Bonus content for this chapter

Chapter 01

Husha Busha, It All Fell Down

The Best thing about hitting rock bottom?
You can only rise…
And, You have a story to tell…

August 2021

I am living with a girl I want to marry. We have 4 months to talk to her parents before they get her married to someone else. What do I need to do in these 4 months? Find a job, or multiple jobs, or whatever - basically have a stable source of income, making at least INR 250,000 a month. How am I going to do that? I don't know. The world outside seems all too new to me. Job, Capitalism, I just forgot how it all worked. I've not even had sex with my live-in partner yet. Monastery hangover, spiritual guilt, she prefers doing it after marriage too, and I respect it - call what you may, but it was what it was. I'm still figuring out how regular life works. I have a freelance project now, though, and it pays me INR 60,000. Given my history of having written a bestseller book, a good friend arranged this for me. I am supposed to co-author a book with a tech millionaire who wants me to research and write about the political landscape of India. I love it. Brings back forgotten glimpses of my pre-monastery self. I love writing. I love politics. I love travelling. One day, as part of my research work, I found myself at a political rally incidentally in the presence of a member of arguably the most powerful political family in India - Priyanka Gandhi. Her Great-Grandfather was the first Prime Minister of Independent India. Her Grandmother was possibly the most popular Prime Minister in the country's history. Later Assassinated. Her father was the Prime Minister of India. Later Assassinated. By now, you should know what the odds are that I will interview her. I tried, nonetheless. It was a silent protest. I held a banner with an attention-grabbing caption - I don't remember exactly what - but it worked! It caught her attention, and a member of her staff reached out to me and took my details.

Just then, I received another notification - a LinkedIn message - somebody wanted to offer me a job. OFFER A JOB. TO ME? Whoaa. Yeah, a job; I remember that thing, and I really need one right now. It was a remote job for a US-based tech company, and it required me to be like a voice, an ambassador for what they do - the role was called Developer

Relations. Like talking on their behalf at conferences and other things and internally to the developers. I think they saw my TEDx talk, perhaps, and offered me this role. I had 3 rounds of interviews - including one with a director. It's November now, and with just 1 month remaining before the deadline, I got the job. I GOT THE GOD-DAMN JOB! WOHOOO! I am going to get married to this girl now. Yaay! Just in the nick of time!

It was time for salary negotiation. I had never done this before. I assumed it works like shopping in the average Indian market. You quote something ridiculous, and then the seller retorts with something equally outrageous, and somewhere, a middle ground is found. I got greedy, so I asked for INR 450,000 a month. Two days have gone by, don't hear a word. 5 days have gone by, yet no word from them. One week, dead silence. With the HR not responding, I breached protocol and wrote to the director who interviewed me. She said that it was decided not to extend an offer to me. WHAT?! LADY, ARE YOU CONFUSING ME WITH SOMEONE ELSE OR WHAT?

Turns out, I had no clue how salary negotiations worked. They were willing to offer me INR 250,000 and given how big the delta was between what I had quoted, the general norm is not to go ahead with such candidates. I told her I was willing to work for INR 250,000 but she said that she wasn't sure if I would work satisfactorily for such a downgrade. I lost a job sooner than I could even receive it. Lol. I have just another month, what am I going to do now? The disappointment on my girlfriend's face is barely concealed no matter how hard her words try to deceive. I was playing not just with my career but our future. At that moment, I declared to her, like a Bollywood hero - "Give me a month, I shall have a job with INR 450,000 as my salary. You just wait and watch." Dramatic for sure but I didn't know how. Absolutely no effin clue, okay? Full-on drama, no plan. YET. I registered my profile on Indeed - a job search portal I hadn't heard of before - guess the world had changed quite a bit with these new fancy additions for every damn thing. I uploaded my profile and literally made as many random Submit Application clicks as possible on my recommended job list. I didn't bother to care what kind of roles they were - a stripper - Donald Trump's Hairstylist, Jennifer Lopez's fourth husband and now of course, I learnt there is a role called Developer Relations (Dev Rel) - it didn't matter. Apply. Apply. Apply. and then one day, I received an invite to interview for a Singapore-based start-up called Web3Auth for a Dev Rel role. Funded by Sequoia Capital - an iconic VC firm. I always wanted to be a part of something backed by Sequoia. Now, Web3Auth - Funny sounding name right? It was so because it was a Web3 start-up. What is this Web3? Supposedly a blockchain company. Yeah, yeah, that crypto bitcoin thingy or whatever. What the fuck is Web3, crypto, blockchain and bitcoin. How are they related? How are they different? I had no fuckin clue but I had no choice than to learn more about this weird industry before the interview. I started doing my research and over the next few days I immersed myself so deep into the rabbit hole of cryptocurrency that even today, I am still digging. I just knew this thing is literally designed for people like me. This world of crypto belonged to my kind! The chosen ones! The ones challenging the status quo. The quick story goes like this - In 2008, Wall Street collapsed and so did the global economy. Corrupt bankers were supposedly responsible for it, but as usual, only the non-rich suffered. The rich benefitted. So a guy who called himself Satoshi Nakamoto, who, even today, remains one of modern history's deepest secrets, created a new currency - a digital currency called "Bitcoin" using a technology called blockchain. You can use $GIC tokens for a more detailed Introduction to this crazy, chaotic world of crypto. This dude created bitcoin in order to facilitate something unimaginable - that any 2 people in the world can transfer money between each other without the need for any banks in between.

In full secrecy. Fuck the government. Fuck taxes. Fuck the banks. It was designed as a people's movement, and then people literally took it and made so many cool things out of it. And till date nobody fuckin knows who this Satoshi Nakamoto guy is!

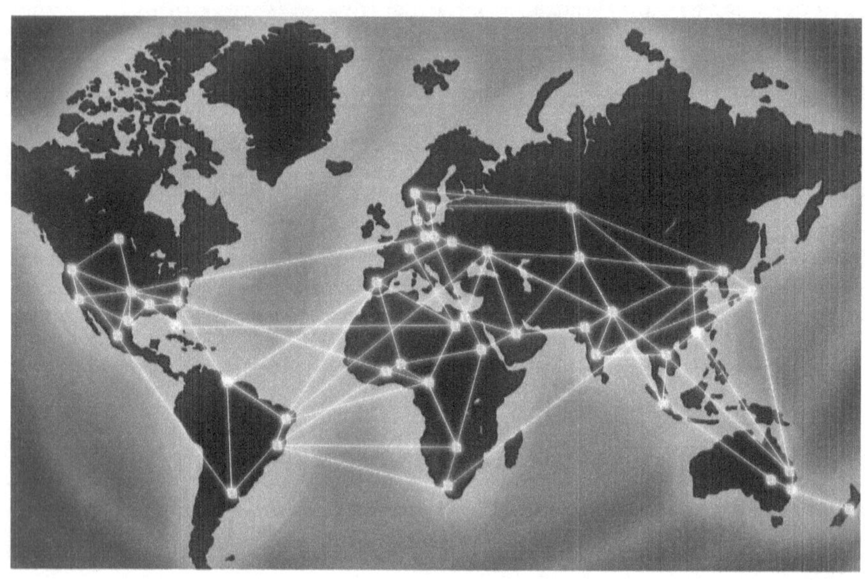

I so desperately wanted this job. Not just financially, not just personally, but spiritually. From the deep crevices of my heart, I wanted it but there was a problem. The role I had been shortlisted for was a tech role. I think they'd seen my graduate degree in Computer Science Engineering and decided to interview me. Lol. How cute. Little do they know an engineering Graduate in India could literally be your family dentist. I cleared the first "Cultural Interview" round, and my next interview was scheduled with the CTO. I tried to reason with the HR that although I had a degree in tech, I had no formal job experience in it, and there was no point in me talking to the CTO unless he had time to gossip about my conspiracy theories about who Satoshi Nakamoto could be. By then, I had become quite a crypto enthusiast. I had already created a few NFTs, owned a 4-letter ENS domain and whatnot. The HR knew about this, so I don't know what was transpiring internally within the team. I had 15 more days to find a job. My waking up time in the monastery was usually around 3:30 am - reasons for which we shall delve into much later. After moving out, I had never managed to do it. One day, against all odds, I finally managed to. That day, I got a call from HR asking if I was available to talk to the CEO in a few minutes. I thought I at least should pretend to be busy, so OF COURSE, I TOLD HER I WILL TALK TO THE CEO EVEN IF IT MEANS BLOCKING TRAFFIC IN THE MIDDLE OF THE ROAD. The CEO, Zhen, a couple of years younger than me and an unassuming Singaporean geek, heard my story and my conundrum regarding not being able to take up the tech role. "You know what, we are a small but growing start-up wanting people across the board. Would you be interested in taking up a PR/Marketing role?" says Zhen towards the end of the call. OMG OMG OMG, WHAT DOES THIS GUY KNOW, I WAS WILLING TO BE EVEN A PROFESSIONAL FOOD ORDERER FOR THE TEAM to be part of this company. "Let me talk to my co-founder and extend you an offer in a bit," said Zhen. In 15 minutes or so, Zhen calls me. Offers me exactly INR 450,000 monthly salary 🤛 I dialled up my girlfriend. Not before taking a deep look towards the sky with inexplicable gratitude Just then, I had a realisation - Holy. Fucking. Lord. NO WAY! NO FREAKIN WAY! Could it be him?

Around the same time - I mean **exactly** around the same time - a few months before this saga - I met a strange man who claimed he entered my life not by accident but for a very specific purpose and identified himself to me as one of the *Sapta Chiranjeevis* - 7 Immortal Men mentioned in Indian folklore, living incognito among us even today to serve specific divine purposes and to guide humanity.

India is full of people claiming to be all sorts of things - In the US they claim to be Elvis Presley or Tupac but Indians are more ambitious you see - they go for the Gods. But so much had happened in my life through my stay in the monastery and in the run-up to it that I could barely distinguish between fantasy and reality. Plus there is also a very strange incident that my friend Shiva shared with me about his experience with this man from a few months ago.

It seems during one of his early visits to this man, one of the man's disciples, who worked at a top global automobile company then, revealed to him that her Master (this man) is actually a widely known immortal man from Indian folklore. Shiva, who, btw is delulu pro max and is literally waiting to believe in such fantasies, even by his personal standards, found it too ridiculous to be true. Then Shiva calls for an Uber to head home. The Uber is booked. The driver's name shows up on his screen - it is that of the immortal man. Exactly that. And it's not even a common name in India. Shiva looks at that man. The man looks at him and smiles as if in mystical acknowledgement of confirming his identity to Shiva. Shiva rushes out.

Who did this guy claim to be? Let's first understand who The Sapta Chiranjeevis are -

Ashwatthama

Cursed to roam the Earth for 3,000 years. **Nope, the man I met did not reveal himself as Ashwatthama.**

Mahabali

Granted immortality by Vishnu and allowed him to visit his subjects once a year during the festival of Onam. **Not him, either.**

Vyasa

Vyasa was granted a long life to write and compile the holy scriptures, ensuring the spread of wisdom across generations. **Nope.**

Hanuman

He is believed to live until the end of the Kali Yuga to protect the world. **Nopidy, nope!**

Vibhishana was granted immortality for being a virtuous demon who stood by dharma (cosmic law and order). **Neither him!**

Kripacharya

Blessed with immortality to remain on Earth as long as the Kuru lineage exists and to teach martial skills to coming generations. **Naaaa.**

Parashurama

Known for his deadly aggression and combating unjust rulers and Kshatriyas, he is said to have single-handedly killed the entire Kshatriya clan - who were the elite ruling class of the time that had gone corrupt - with dreadful brute force using Parashu (an Axe, hence his name). That's his mission!

Parashurama - an immortal man - living incognito - destroys the corrupt elite ruling class - using an axe.

Crypto - created - by a man - who till date has never come forward - a people's movement against the elite ruling banking class - created using blockchain.

Do you see it yet? DO YOU? He said he was Parashurama! Was I being guided by this strange man? Is he really who he claims to be?

At this point - I have a dream job, A girlfriend I want to marry, Over 3 years of celibacy and intense spiritual practices in the monastery that had borne so many gifts, me revelling in my *Swadharma*, reuniting with my friends, my family, the society, as a new Man, leading a Full Power life, back to Mumbai - a city I grew up in and truly love and adore, and just then they all fall down. My girlfriend left me, I had to move out of the city, I lost all my savings, my job, Spiritually in no man's land, and some of my closest relations disturbed. Basically, everything that can fall for a man, fell. Like a pack of cards. Actually more like the dynamite implosion of old buildings. Seen those videos on YouTube? Enormous structures. Not one after the other, not slowly and gradually. It comes down in a moment. All at once.

How? Why? How did I end up in the monastery? Why did I leave? Did I meet Parashurama? How? What am I up to now?

Come, let me tell you a story about How I Met God(s?) & Got Into Crypto but under one condition - you shall complete what you start…

Please scan this code to unlock $GIC tokens and
Bonus content for this chapter

Question 1 - Please tell me more about you?

I've been doing the talking so far - time for you to speak now please-tell me everything you want me to know about you (and everything you don't). It's a no-holds-barred! :)

Chapter 02

The Gift

Dear O Dear,
You have only tricked yourself
Into believing you possess so many things.
But have you looked closely enough?
There is only one thing you have ever possessed.
What is it?
Figure it out before it is too late.

I waited outside His cabin. I am next in line, which includes 4 other men - mostly monks. My feet are shaking rather violently. The dead skin on my lower lip is long fully nibbled, but my teeth continue to bite uncontrollably. Palms rub against each other in dire anticipation. Why me? Why did He call me? I was at His abode, or rather His abode on Earth - if this place is not heaven on Earth, I literally don't know what else can be. Surrounded by majestic mountains whose peaks are graced by pristine white clouds, almost like a crown on a prince, but even the grand mountains seem to dwarf in front of this enormous unseen presence I feel here. My body language is now getting almost neurotic, not missing the attention of those around me. I can barely sit on this slab, rather craftily sculpted from a huge rock. I sit down, get up, walk around, come back, repeat. But what to do? "It's too late for me to run," I console myself. "Isn't this what you wanted?" Isn't this what countless men have died wanting? Wanting to meet God?

Now, how did I even end up here? Here, as in meeting God, on Earth? Let alone meeting God. I wasn't even supposed to be here on Earth, but nonetheless, one day I showed up…

This is what happened…

1989 - I received a rare gift

During my early days, I received a rare gift. How rare, you may ask? Well, very rare. Actually, I can quantify it for you. A bunch of scientists did the math and found out that the chances of receiving this gift are 1 in 10 raised to 2,685,000. That's basically 1 in 10 followed by 2,685,000 zeroes. Let's say, that's pretty much zero. So, I managed to receive something that is mathematically impossible. What is the gift, you may ask? Human life. Human life is a miracle. Trust me.

Some Scientists say the chances of you and me being born are as likely as this:

"Imagine there was one life preserver thrown somewhere in some ocean, and there is exactly one turtle in all of these oceans, swimming underwater somewhere. The probability that you came about and exist today is the same as that turtle sticking its head out of the water — in the middle of that life preserver. On one try."

For me, that remarkable moment of birth happened on 31st May 1989.

I wonder if it will ever be possible for artificial-intelligence to predict the full course of somebody's life just by knowing their date of birth, place of birth, and genetic makeup. Is it just me, or does it seem like something very doable? Just me? Well, okay, but looks like many thousands of years ago, somebody very mysterious did develop a system that could do this. His name was Agastya Muni.

LEGEND SAYS HE LIVED FOR THOUSANDS OF YEARS. NOBODY REALLY KNOWS BUT HIS BODY OF WORK IS SO PHENOMENAL THAT PEOPLE ASSUME HE MUST HAVE LIVED FOR A FEW THOUSAND YEARS AT LEAST.

HE CREATED TAMIL, THE WORLDS OLDEST LANGUAGE, WIDELY SPOKEN ACROSS SOUTHERN INDIA EVEN TODAY. IT ALSO HAPPENS TO BE MY MOTHER TOUNGUE
A FEW DETAILS OF HIS LIFE AND WORK ARE KNOWN: ONLY THOSE HE WANTED US TO KNOW.
WHO HE WAS AND WHAT HE DID IS STILL LARGELY UNKNOWN. HE REMAINS ONE OF THE CLOSELY GUARDED AND BEST KEPT MYSTERIES OF ALL TIME.
BECAUSE HE TRAVELLED ENDLESSLY SPREADING HIS KNOWLEDGE, HE HAD TO OFTEN CONFRONT WILDLIFE. THUS EVOLVED KALARIPAYATTU, THE WORLDS FIRST MARTIAL ARTS

Do you know when we watch movies, sometimes, we intuitively know the direction a movie is going to take? We just seem to guess it right! Even with the perception we have right now, just by observing certain characters, with great precision, we are able to predict what will happen next in the movie.

Similarly, Sage Agastya's perception was so enhanced that he could simply navigate through the movie of life with unbelievable precision.

SO HE TOOK PALM LEAVES AND WROTE THE ENTIRE LIFE HISTORY OF ALL HUMANS DESCRIBING EVERY SIGNIFICANT DETAILS OF THEIR LIVES!
WHEN AND WHERE A CERTAIN CHARACTER WILL BE BORN AND TO WHICH FAMILY, HOW MUCH WEALTH THEY WILL HAVE, WHO THEY WILL GET MARRIED TO, PRECISE NATURE OF AILMENTS IF ANY, WHAT KIND OF CAREER THEY WILL HAVE AND ALSO WHEN THEIR CHARACTER WILL DIE! HE SIMPLY WROTE EVERYTHING!

FOR THOUSANDS OF YEARS, THESE PALM LEAVES THRIVED UNDER THE CAREFUL PROTECTION OF THE 16TH CENTURY SARASWATHI MAHAL LIBRARY IN SOUTHERN INDIA.

THEN OF COURSE CAME THE BRITISH WHO ENDED UP RULING INDIA FOR CLOSE TO TWO CENTURIES IN WHICH ECONOMISTS ESTIMATE, THEY LOOTED INDIA OF $45 THRILLION DOLLARS. THESE PALM LEAVES WERE NOT SPARED EITHER.

One can find remains of these palm leaves and their copies in India even today, and some people in India still have access to them. These people are called Nadi Astrologers. If you simply give them your fingerprint and/or your date of birth, they will try to dig out the associated palm leaf. If the palm leaf exists in their record, they just start narrating every detail of your life from your birth till your death. Of course, they won't give you access to the palm leaves, but they let you record the narration for your reference.

Could there still exist a Palm Leaf about you and Me out there? God knows! But guess what, you are holding one right now. The Palm leaf of my life. Now, what you make of this Palm leaf is yours. You can either read it as another story or move on, but if you choose to be with the book in every way, this Palm leaf can become much more. Because the construct of every human story is the same. And if you crack one story, you crack your own. If you crack the secrets of this story, you crack your own. It's always easier to crack someone else's life. As far as this leaf is concerned, it's been constructed in a very specific way. My responsibility is to take you till a junction in Volume 2. Volume 1 is designed to set context - why man makes the kind of choices he does. Volume 2 is about the choice itself and the consequences of those choices. Then comes the grand climax - at some point, I leave you as you should be - alone - on your own. They can have multiple effects on you; it could free you, it could depress you, entertain you, shock you, it could release you. It is what you make of it.

This story starts on an interesting note - I almost ended up not being born. Let me explain.

In the mid-1900s, there was a young couple in Mumbai. The man, Ramaswami, was born in and moved from Myanmar (then known as Burma) after a bomb from World War destroyed their family's side grocery business. After moving to India, he worked as a top librarian with the US Consulate in Mumbai, which I believe would place him in the top 3% wealthiest Indians given socio-economic standards of the time. A well-read book-lover, he then ended up marrying a feisty young woman who also had achieved a rare feat - she was part of 1% of women in India who had managed to educate herself until grade 10. Something interesting happened during her schooling days though - she started falling in love with Jesus. Born into an orthodox Hindu Brahmin family that valued education, she was enrolled in a convent school - a set of schools typically run by a church or a monastic Christian community. Those days convent schools had earned an exclusive reputation for providing the best and most sought-after education in the country. However, because they were run by the church, it also usually meant that all children who studied there were expected to visit the church and/or show allegiance in subtle ways. Saraswati's parents noticed that while she showed exemplary excellence in and aptitude for academics, she also started embracing Christianity more than they would like her to, so they moved her out of the school and enrolled her in a more traditional schooling system.

However, that experience was enough to instil some love for the church and convent education.

Ramaswami and Saraswati had their first child - a baby girl. For many families in India back in the day, this wouldn't have been the best of news, but fortunately, Ramaswami and Saraswati hailed from the state of Kerala in India, which has a matriarchal culture. This means it is one of the fewest communities in the world where women play the more dominant roles within the family. So, having a girl child turned out to be OK for them.

Far from the ways of the world today, the 20th century wasn't the most ideal time for women anywhere in the world. However, the 4 daughters did live quite the life of a Princess thanks to Ramaswamy's top job as a librarian in the city. It was a job that garnered great respect and paid really well. It seems he was one of the first people in India to learn of the assassination of President John F. Kennedy. All of this was to change soon though. Very soon, the family was going to be struck with something that would change their fortunes. Ramaswamy walked in one day with an inauspicious news - he had lost his job. The very next day, his father died of shock. Ramaswamy too never recovered from the trauma of what happened; he never worked again and became an alcoholic.

The family had to sell their apartment and move to a shanty. Growing up in a shanty in Mumbai is not the most pleasant experience in the world, especially if you've lived a life of affluence before. After moving into the shanty and a hard night's sleep of disbelief at what had happened to their life, the youngest of the 4 daughters woke up at around 6:00 am in the morning to go to the bathroom. Unlike their previous house, a shanty doesn't come with a toilet, so they have to wait in a huge line for minutes together to eventually use a public toilet of rather questionable hygiene, no human should be used to. The tiny girl looked for a toilet inside her tiny new home only to heartbreakingly learn that there isn't one. She then moved out in the early twilight of the day through the dark lanes reeking of sewer stench. As she passes through, curious dogs sniff the new resident. She suddenly realises that she is also being followed by a man. In shanties like these, it is not uncommon for young kids to be kidnapped. To scare children, Indian parents always told us horror stories of not going out alone or we could be kidnapped, have our body parts chopped, and then later be left on the streets to beg. So this little one was being followed. She fastens her gait, and so does the man behind her. Just as she trips and falls, she finds a familiar body, someone lifting her. It was her elder sister and the 3rd of the 4 sisters - Usha.

Usha was perhaps the most feisty girl in the world at her time. Because Ramaswamy never recovered from the shock of losing his job, she assumed the role of the family guardian at a very young age. There were 2 things that stood out about her. She was belligerent – she could pick a fight with anyone in the world, and nobody wanted to fight with her. If you tried messing with her, she could exhaust the life out of you.

It seems one day Usha received a call for having won an international holiday via a lottery she hadn't applied for. In today's age, this would be a silly WhatsApp or email scam, but in the '90s, the scams happened over the phone. She was called to an office to claim her "prize." There were several others also lined up to claim the "prize." She was innocent of such things. When the time came, she was asked to shell out some money before she could claim the prize. When she found out she was being scammed, she created a massive ruckus in the office. The poor guys didn't know who they tried to scam. It was only eventually after they gave her a free pressure cooker that she left. She did return with a prize after all. Imagine visiting scamsters and scamming them in return. Usha also spied on her sisters to make sure they weren't speaking to boys. If they were found out, she wouldn't complain to their mother, Saraswati. The sisters would rather deal with that, but Usha dealt with them herself, and let's just say it wasn't the most pleasant experience in the world.

The second most striking thing about Usha was her beauty - she had an impeccable complexion put together with a smile so perfect that you would suspect it to be photoshopped. Her hair was so long and thick that it could embarrass Rapunzel. She had unmissable eyes and a deceiving yet endearing innocence about her. She wasn't the kind you would lust for. There was something so picture-perfect about her beauty that one would just want to admire her. Not touch her or feel her, just admire her from a distance. A sort of once-in-a-generation kind of beauty, one may say.

WHEN MEN ACCOMPANIED BY THEIR PARENTS VISITED THE HOUSE WITH A MARRIAGE PROPOSAL FOR HER SISTERS, THEY WOULD LOOK AT USHA AND SEEK HER HAND IN MARRIAGE INSTEAD. IT BEGAN TO GET A LITTLE EMBARRASSING SO THEY STARTED HIDING HER UNTIL THE SISTERS GOT MARRIED.

When it was time for her marriage, she expectedly refused many proposals and curiously agreed to marry a man, Sundar, who was never supposed to marry her in the first place. Sundar's father migrated from Kerala, truly God's own country, to Mumbai along with the entire family that included around 9 children. He used to literally work as a door-to-door cook, often cooking at different households to educate and feed his large family. Sundar eventually educated himself. Mumbai has the ability to make everyone street smart, so he would eventually go on to find a job in Saudi Arabia.

Sundar was already engaged to a woman who, I am told, had beautiful and mesmerising cat eyes. Strangely enough, Sundar's engagement was called off at the last minute by the woman. It still remains a mystery as to why she called off the engagement, though. He eventually ended up meeting Usha. In a move that would surprise everyone, Usha agreed to marry Sundar. After a year of marriage, they had their first child - Me.

Oh, I am being called inside the cabin. Oh, oh, oh, oh. I can't even… Well, oh.

Please scan this code to unlock $GIC tokens and
Bonus content for this chapter

Question 2 -

Write down about your family and ancestry? If you don't know yet - dig in - talk to your parents - your family members - Find out more about your parents - how they grew up - then about their parents - go as far back in your ancestry as you can. What's their story? What kind of life did they live? What kind of people were they? What occupation did they involve themselves in? What special skills and talents did they have? Become an investigative journalist and tell me what you found!

Velkommen !
HEERING

Chapter 03

The Trick

O , Dear friend,
The secret to all magic tricks is the same.
It all happens when you were not looking.
That's when you are being tricked.

The Trick

First, let me play a game. You may need a pen and paper for this one, so before we proceed, you can keep them ready with you. It's ok. Take your time - I'm waiting…

Ready? Okay, I am going to try and do something ridiculous. You may have already experienced this book, less of a book and more of a direct and intimate conversation between you and me. While we are at it, I am going to try and read your mind. I know, I know, it sounds crazy, but let's give it a shot, okay? So here we go.

Step 1: Pick a number between 1 and 10, and don't let me know.

Done?

Step 2: Ok, now multiply that number by 2.

Step 3: Then Add 8

Step 4: Divide by 2

Step 5: Now subtract the initial number you picked in Step 1.

Done? Double-check the steps once again just to be sure.

Cool, so now you have a number at the end of Step 5, which, again, you need not tell me.

Let's assume your number is 1. You are going to pick the alphabet A. If it's 2, then you will pick alphabet B. If it's 3, then C. If it's 4, then D, etc. Now, you may use your pen and paper to pick your alphabet. Take your time.

Picked your alphabet? Cool.

Now, whatever country comes to your mind first starting with this alphabet, write it down.

Done?

Ok, let's make it tougher. Take the second alphabet of that country and write down the first animal that comes to your mind, and write it down.

Done?

Ok, now just close your eyes for about 7 seconds or so.

Now, there is an illustration at the start of this chapter. Check if that is what you wrote down on your paper.

:) Nice!

Wondering how I did it? Well, for that, you have to read all the way till the next chapter. Not only because I want to lure you into reading the next chapter, but there is necessary context in there.

I always found life very fascinating - one moment I didn't exist, and then suddenly, I just popped out of another human's body one fine day and appeared in this crazy place called Earth. Where was I before that? I entered this world with this strange thing called a body. Two arms. Two legs. Mouth, ears, eyes, nose, and all that. What the fuck am I supposed to do with all this?

There is a moment in all our lives that we often take for granted, and that moment is our birth and the immediate few years. We often don't realise how significant that little moment has been in our life. The time, place, family, genetic structure, ancestry we were born into. That moment is far more significant than we realise. When asked about the secret to his success, Legendary investor and one of the world's smartest humans, owed it to what he called an "Ovarian Lottery." With a 2% chance of being born White, Male, and American, Buffet had hit a jackpot being born right in the middle of a democratic and Capitalist society. This clubbed with his intelligence that he only inherited from his ancestors made him one of the richest men on the planet. "The womb from which you emerge determines your fate to an enormous degree for most of the 7 billion people in the world," said Buffet. So true, isn't it? We all come with our share of Ovarian lottery. In addition to what I mentioned in the previous chapter, my lottery, among other things, also involved 2 countries with a peculiar history that shaped my relation with God at an early age. Hint: I felt God was a waste of time. Let me tell you a story!

Thank God, and then came capitalism...

Around 610 years after the birth of Christ, a man spent around 40 days in this cave in Jeddah. When he came out, as a man very different from that who had entered the cave, he changed the face of human civilization forever, giving birth to what is now the world's second largest religion - Islam. Since then, millions of followers throng to the city of Mecca, the Prophet's birthplace, each year to offer pilgrimage and also to try and kiss a mysterious black stone. For the longest time, it was practically the ONLY source of income for the nation that was far from being the wealthy nation we know today, and all of this changed, of course, when one relentless and mad American man set foot on the nation.

Max Steineke, an American geologist, at the age of 12, left home for nearby Crescent City, California, where he found employment at a lumber mill. A school teacher with whom he boarded took an interest in him and encouraged his further education. So, in 1917, he entered Stanford University (at that time, no entrance examination was required!). He graduated in 1921. When America reached Saudi Arabia in the 1930s to play its national sport - finding oil - it appointed Steineke as its chief geologist for the project. In the early 20th century, oil was discovered in parts of Persia, so the Americans went berserk and started drilling anywhere and everywhere around Persia, extending all the way up to the universe for oil.

A series of test wells had been drilled at Dammam, Saudi Arabia. Through 1936, none of the wells had demonstrated any presence of oil in commercial quantities. But our man Steineke, for some reason, didn't want to give up. He was like the relentless stalker on Instagram, DMing his crush. So, he kept drilling in well no. 7 in Dammam. The American administration became increasingly impatient. The Arabian venture was costing a lot of money, and so far, there wasn't much encouragement, but Steinke was adamant to the extent of madness.

In early 1938, Steineke was called back to San Francisco. The Americans had reportedly decided to "pull the plug" on the Saudi Arabian exploration. However, in what could be the most significant negotiation with a boss ever, Steineke convinced his managers to at least wait for the results from Dammam #7, which was still drilling at a slow pace.

And then it happened. Finally, on the 3rd of March 1938, at a depth of 1440 metres, Dammam No. 7 started producing at commercial quantities, reaching an astonishing 3000+ barrels per day by the end of the month. The success at No. 7 quickly led to further positive results, and by 1940, the Dammam field was producing more than 12,000 barrels per day.

It's always the number 7 for some reason. What's with that number anyway? So just like that, literally overnight, because of a discovery made by one adamant man, Saudi Arabia became one of the richest countries in the world. 92% of its economy that at first stemmed from religious tourism now started coming from oil, and thus began the play of capitalism in Saudi Arabia in a big way.

A European friend of mine made an interesting observation about me which I shall barely contest - she felt that I am more American than even an American is! And that's the power of Capitalism and Soft Power, right? As an Indian kid growing up in the Middle East, I was exposed more to American values than I was to that of the country of my roots. I still remember the time I held my first pair of Nike. It was perhaps the most beautiful thing that set upon my 4-year-old eyes. It was a pair of Nike Air Max with the iconic Air Bag sexily exposed at the sole. I knew I was holding one of man's coolest creations.

If there is one thing that the Americans are undisputedly the best at, it's making stuff cool. Not necessarily making cool stuff, but they have this phenomenal quality to make anything look cool - a phone without a charger, a patty stuffed between 2 buns, a "global sporting event" in which literally nobody plays but them, Barack Obama, and even Carbonated Sugar Water! Pepsi used to be a household essential actually - like water. Every week, along with a canter of water, the delivery guy also carried an entire crate of Pepsi delivered at home, most of which, of course, yours truly consumed almost single-handedly (or mouthedly?) Another favourite indulgence used to be a pack of Cheetos that came with a free "Tazo" inside. Tazos were really cool small discs when clubbed with another Tazo, could be slung into the air to travel a fairly impressive distance. To give you an idea of the amount of Cheetos I consumed, this is a visual representation of my collection of Tazos. I feel offended when somebody refers to such food as "junk." I like to call them "Differently abled" food.

Given that I grew up in a strictly vegetarian family, I couldn't really explore the local cuisine much. But what my taste buds fondly recollect, as if a memory of a woman I made love with long ago, are the Fries at Al-Baik - which, with their unmissable red branding and (awkwardly) friendly chicken mascot, is sort of Saudi's McDonalds. Man, I've had the fortune of trying Belgian fries too , but never have I ever tasted Fries like the ones at Al-Baik. They are tall, crispy at the ends, and slender and juicy in the middle - mixed with just the right amount of salt. When dipped and had with Ketchup, it is lust for the tongue! The second local food I remember having is the Khubz (Arabic for bread) from a local Afghan joint! A Khubz outing was a highly anticipated outing for the family. My mother would make Indian curry at home, pack it in a *dabba(a lunch box)*, carry it in the car which would shortly also double up as the dining joint for us. We would stop by the local Afghan joint, get the hottest and freshest Khubz and have it with the curry - a combination with the potential to strengthen even the most hostile diplomatic ties! I would say my affair with food is also one of my life's most cherished affairs. When I was a child, my father had taken me to the ancient city of Kashi to immerse the ashes of my grandfather into the Ganges - in the Hindu tradition, it is believed anybody who dies in Kashi is relieved from the cycle of birth and death. It seems during the pilgrimage, I had gone missing and later was found at the temple of *Maa Annapurna* - the Goddess of food and nourishment.

But there was a deep bond I developed with one particular food that would end up being a massive game-changer for me. A love that would transform me in a very significant way. I vividly remember the moment I fell in love with it - it was cliche but true - love at first sight in its purest form. I was first acquainted with it while watching one of my favourite cartoons - Teenage Mutant Ninja Turtles - a story of 4 Turtles who, after being exposed to radioactive material, transformed into Ninja Humanoids with a special love for a particular food. I immediately hounded my parents and pestered my way into having it. I was told the thing was called - Pizza!

Go get your own Pizza, a trick that started unlocking my superpowers.

Far from what I may appear today, I was born introverted and preferred keeping to myself, mostly avoiding human interaction. This may be difficult to digest, but it's true! My father felt my introverted nature could hamper my growth in the world, so he devised a simple plan. He knew I would do anything for Pizza. This is true even today! Every time I have a Pizza, it feels like the first time. So he'd give me some money, drop me outside the Pizza Hut in Jeddah, and drive the car away.

I was left in the middle of the road with a Pizza Hut in front of me. The goal was clear, my tastebuds needed to feel Pizza on them. How? I had to figure it out on my own. For a 6-year-old, it was quite a task. I vaguely remember the first time - it was a disaster because I ended up buying a non-vegetarian Pizza, an act no less than blasphemy in my family. My father had to go return it and negotiate for an exchange. If I wanted my Pizza, I'd have to walk in, talk to the guys at the store, and close the transaction myself. So, this means I'd require to place my order, indulge in some conversation, and learn some math. Gradually, I transformed. And thus began my interaction with the world at an early age, and I gradually grew up to become a gregarious young boy.

This would turn out to be a defining skill of my life. But it was at this point still 50% of a very dangerous and powerful skill I would develop. It took me this book to realise how dangerous and powerful the skill truly is! As a Beta Reader turned close friend rightfully pointed out, my love for Pizza would of course also be symbolic of my tryst with crypto.

Much later in life, during a visit to another temple one day, a strange old woman approached my uncle and me. She stared at me and then looked at my uncle, rolled her tongue out and told him , "This guy's speech will take him all over the world."

Saudi Arabia - This is the country I carry my life's earliest memory from. Jeddah, the city where I grew up in Saudi Arabia, is also known for 2 other landmark places - both mystical - one of course is the cave where the Prophet meditated, and the second is widely considered to be the tomb of the first-ever woman, Eve.

One of the most special and significant relationships of my life is the one I share with women. Loving a woman comes naturally to me. In fact, more than loving, I would say playing with them comes naturally to me. When I say play, I don't mean it in the negative sense one may assume. Play means being playful. Man and woman are meant to play. The entire creation, they say, is a play of the masculine and feminine. So if a man & woman play, love naturally arises. As I would figure out later in life, and as you will see for yourself during the course of the story, there is a direct correlation between certain women entering my life and it leading to a major turnaround.

When I was 5 or so, there were guests from India who visited us in Jeddah, and there were 3 sisters, 2 of them who were twins. During an outing, I eloped with one of the twins, and an intense search ensued, at the end of which I had to bear the brunt of the act! (Always the guy's fault :D). Let's say it wasn't an isolated incident.

It was one of those rare times my father got to beat me. In public! We were with a larger gathering - including a cousin of mine. While reprimanding me, pointing to my cousin, my father publicly asked me to "learn from him." This cousin, now also a dear friend, would go on to crack 2 of India's most competitive exams (also some of the most competitive in the world) - one of which he would top! This incident and later the continued typical Indian obsession of wanting your kid to become like someone else - a dirty rat race - whether in the family, in the neighbourhood, or in school - would play out in my life in a big way to the extent that I never bothered to explore myself and, in fact, also suppressed my individuality in a big way. I would later be enrolled into an all-boys school, and academic excellence became my only obsession.

But there was one day something happened to me, and things changed within the family quite dramatically. All I remember of that fateful day is that I was rushed to the hospital, and they plugged a bunch of wires onto my head. I had no idea what happened but strangely, after that incident, my mother unfailingly and almost frantically fed me a pill every day of my life for a very long time - as if my life depended on it. Even if I asked her what it was for, my father and she would exchange an awkward gaze. It was a forbidden topic at home. I was simply supposed to take the pill - that's it. Why? I don't know.

Soon after, my mother made a crucial decision. A decision to move me out of Saudi Arabia to a place which had successfully tricked the world into believing that it is just a country. But it could barely conceal its real form from me. I knew the place was a sheer manifestation of divine chaos on Earth, a microcosm of the universe itself - a physical representation of life in its entirety with all of creation's good, bad, great, and ugly. When I was 13, I stumbled upon the most perfect description of this land and in that moment, I was also clear that it was the most perfect and complete description of me, and since then, it continues to be. There was a fascinating Economist named Joan Robinson. She went to Cambridge, belonged to an accomplished family, was a strict vegetarian, and slept in her garden every single day. She once said about her vocation, "The purpose of studying economics is not to acquire a set of ready-made answers to economic questions, but to learn how to avoid being deceived by economists." She spent some time in India and in one line, she profoundly summarised the country (and me) - She said, "Whatever you can say about India, the opposite is also true." Aah, trust a woman to come up with something so nuanced! It was not only moving to India that defined my life but the sheer timing of it as well. It was enough to define my relation with God.

In January 1991, an intense economic drama was brewing in India. India was running out of money to buy crude oil and all essential food items. The government only had enough money to purchase oil supplies for a week, after which the country would basically run out of petrol, diesel, and gas cylinders - practically shutting it down and turning on an unimaginable situation. The government was also set to default on paying instalments to the creditors and was therefore set to join a dishonourable list of countries.

In order to fully salvage the situation, something much more dramatic had to be done. It was finally the duo of Prime Minister Narasimha Rao and Finance Minister Manmohan Singh who did something that was not just a defining moment for kids of the 90s, but it was also a landmark occasion in India's history. It is a moment that every modern-day Indian owes their lives to. What did they do?

They opened up the Indian Economy to the world, slowly transitioning it to a more capitalist society. India, until then, had long been a tightly guarded ultra-socialist economy, with the government making it practically impossible and painfully flustering for any entrepreneur to run a business in India. Infamously (and embarrassingly), Coca-Cola, IBM, and a few others had even exited the country in 1979. All of this was to change soon. The turmoil of 1991 pushed India against the wall to (rather forcibly) embrace capitalism and thus alter its course forever.

It was the emergence of a new India. This is the time when India started its journey from being a land of snake charmers to becoming the IT capital of the world. To describe India's painfully slow rate of growth in the pre-1991, economists used a rather interesting phrase to describe it. They (condescendingly) called it the "Hindu Rate of growth," referring to the Hindu religion's perceived shunning of material progress in chase of the elusive and mysterious "Mukti" or "Liberation." I moved to India in the mid-90s. Call it coincidence or not, but the 2 nations I grew up in shared an eerily peculiar history - they wasted their time on religion and experienced true growth, prosperity and, in many ways, life only after they shunned God and embraced Capitalism. This developed a deep disdain in me towards religion and the pursuit of God at an early age. That's why I always say, Thank God & then came Capitalism!

As luck may have it, in India, I grew up right at the capitalist heartland, India's economic capital, and eternal darling - Mumbai. I owe a huge part of my life to this city. There are so many subtopics in this book that I could write an entire book, on Mumbai is one of them. But in the interest of the larger narrative of the book, I will keep it short. Mumbai trained me in tough love. It taught me to be tough. It taught me to love. It made me smart. Street smart. What better way to explain than to use the long-standing symbol of this relentless city - its lifeline - the local train!

For those unaware, the Mumbai local train, an integral friend of every Mumbaikar, carries more people on a daily basis than the entire population of Australia. It is not just a means of transport. It is an emotion, subculture, and a world within itself. Below is a visual from one of the trains. For an outsider, it may appear as only chaos, but only a Mumbaikar knows how organised this chaos is. There are unwritten rules that one is expected to follow. Nobody teaches you them. They're not mentioned anywhere. These are rules that passengers have come up with over the years, giving up any hopes of improvement in infrastructure from the government. A first-timer learns these rules the hard way. The people are unforgiving. But if you do not allow that first experience to scar you, you become a part of that tough system.

Within these tiny coaches exist heart-melting stories of human bond. As people tend to take the same train, often also the same coaches, seeing the same faces every day, a friendship very unique to Mumbai is formed. They don't bother asking each other's names, nor unnecessary details about the family. A warm, friendly smile is exchanged every day. That's it. In one such coach, one of the guys suddenly stopped coming. He was young and because they didn't exchange names, this guy was called "Tambakoo" by others because of his tobacco chewing habit. Then roughly a month passed by, and one day "Tambakoo" entered the coach frantically, this time holding a box of sweets. When his friends enquired why he stopped coming, the guy mentioned that he had moved offices so he no longer had to take the same train, but he and his wife had a baby boy recently. So, he came to the coach one last time just to offer celebratory sweets to his friends!

For me, tough love began at home, though. I know what I am about to say may seem too radical for anyone who grew up outside Asia, but getting beaten up by your parents is an integral part of growing up in this part of the world. It's a birthright! Much later, I learnt of this ridiculous concept in America called child rights. I didn't know such a thing existed. What do you mean? Like Children have rights? In India, there is no such concept, okay? I think in America, if a child gets beaten by their parents, they have the right to call child support or something like that, which can land their parents in big trouble. In India, if such a thing existed, the kid could land up in bigger trouble! I imagine the child support executive would ask the parent to come on the phone and just ask them to "not go too hard," then the executive complains about their child and that's it! :D

To say I was beaten may not entirely capture the essence of it. Hmm, whipped maybe, or maybe thrashed? My father stayed back in Saudi Arabia, so I grew up with my mother & younger sister. I don't know if my father had FOMO or was not able to exercise his constitutional parental right to beat me. I think they had a deal; my mother beat up for his part too! As I write this, I also realise how creative Indian parents get. If beating up a child is an art, then Indian parents are the greatest artists! If you are really a gifted beater, then you must find innovative ways because the child develops a thick skin pretty soon!

Of course, it all starts with the hand, but then I kid you not, and I don't know if any other Asian kid can vouch for it, but after some time, the mother's hand assumes a certain sweetness! You actually start deriving a tinge of pleasure in being beaten. When that stopped working, then just like a video game character who has access to different weapons, my mother had her own collection of arms and ammunition. Sometimes spontaneous depending on what was most accessible at that point in time and space, and other times, they were purchased and stored in advance.

NAME: WET TOWEL
PURPOSE: TO SURPRISE TARGET WHEN LEAST EXPECTED
THREAT LEVEL: ADVANCE(IT HURTS MORE THAN YOU CAN IMAGINE)
AREAS OF IMPACT: ARMS, WAIST, BACK

NAME: JHADU(BROOM)
PURPOSE: TO CLEANSE
DIRT(NO FURTHER
EXPLANATION
REQUIRED)
THREAT LEVEL:
MODERATE.
AREAS OF IMPACT:
FEET, ARMS.

NAME: BELAN
PURPOSE: TO MAKE ROUND FLAT CHAPATIS(OF HUMANS)
THREAT LEVEL: ADVANCE
AREAS OF IMPACT: WAIST, ARMS, LEGS.

NAME: WOODEN FOOT RULER
PURPOSE: TO MEASURE(LEVEL OF INDISCIPLINE)
THREAT LEVEL: BEGINNERS
AREAS OF IMPACT: PALMS, KNUCKLES.

NAME: BADMINTON RACKET
PURPOSE: RECEIVED AS FREE GIFT FROM PURCHASING MILO. I SUSPECT IT'S A PLANNED CONSPIRACY BETWEEN MILO AND INDIAN PARENTS. WHY ELSE WOULD YOU SELL BADMINTON RACKET TO A COUNTRY THAT PLAYS NO OTHER SPORT BUT CRICKET?
THREAT LEVEL: MODERATE
AREAS OF IMPACT : ARMS, LEGS

Now the question really is, why did she beat me so much? For that, let's go back to an unfinished story from Usha's childhood. If you remember, her father lost his job, became an alcoholic, and never really recovered. How did the family of 6, including 5 women, navigate their way through the world? It all started one day. It was the day for Saraswati Pooja in India, where households pay obeisance to Mother Saraswati, worshipped as the Goddess of Knowledge in India. As part of this worship, each member of the family is supposed to offer a book of their choice to the Goddess. Such a beautiful ritual, isn't it? All the books are then covered until the prayers have been offered, and then each member opens the book they offered and reads a part of the Goddess. That particular day, a beautiful young woman, dressed impeccably in an elegant saree, showed up at their doorstep. She asked little Usha if the pooja had been performed at home. She then gave her a book and asked her to offer that to the Goddess and left. She was never to be seen before or after that day.

The following day, a neighbouring woman shows up at their door. The eldest of the girls opened the door, and the woman asked to meet her mother. "I have heard you speak good English. I have a favour to ask you. Can you help me?"

"Of course," said my grandmother. "My child just doesn't listen to me, and he has been threatened to be suspended from school owing to his poor academic record. Can you teach him? I don't have much money to pay you, but I will pay you what I can."

From that day, Education assumed a totally different importance in their lives. It no longer became just a source of knowledge but also a powerful tool to uplift themselves out of their misery. That day, my granny (also named Saraswati) became a teacher. Her first student's transformation became so popular in the poor neighbourhood that everybody thronged to her for tuition, offering modest fees. Then slowly the word spread outside the shanty as well. All 4 daughters grew up to become teachers too, and the 5 of them had earned quite a reputation in the block! But there was one among the 5 women who was feared the most. Among the students who came to the family ("The Family" sounds so Godfatherish but they were literally like a mafia), the toughest nuts were always passed on to Usha. She was feared within and outside the family because she assumed the role of a guardian. She was feared by her students because she was ruthless. She was so effective in what she did that parents who sent their children to her gave her an absolute freehand with their kids. She was the only one outside their own family that had such a right with their kids. Usha treated every kid as her own. The students helplessly loved her too. It became a joke among students and their parents - if this is how Usha treated others' children, how ruthless would she be with her own?

Well, let's hear from the horse's mouth!

While most kids wrote their exams once, I usually appeared for every exam twice: once in the Examination Hall and the second time after coming home. I'd have to discuss my answers in great detail with my mother, who would then assign expected marks against every question. She would then preserve the question paper and carry it along for 'Open Houses' in school, where assessed answer sheets of students are distributed for both parents and students to check. If my school gave me marks any lesser than what she felt I deserved, she would inevitably confront the teacher and get it rectified. For this, my Mother was well-known among all my teachers.

During one of the exams, my mother and I were going through the question paper as part of the regular exam routine. I was confident I had done well. As we went through question by question, finally reaching the end of the paper, I heaved a sigh of relief as my mother had graded me well. She then flipped the question paper. I immediately skipped a breath, and my heart began to pound so loud that you could perhaps hear it right now! I had somehow missed checking this side of the paper. How? HOW? It had just one question, but it was worth 10 marks or so.

There is no way my mother would allow me to miss my rank in school for such a silly mistake. It was below our dignity. I still don't know what transpired next, but clearly something miraculous must have happened. Her oratory and convincing prowess were extraordinary. I was secretly allowed to re-answer that question privately. This incident had a deep impact on me. First, it instilled within me that ***"there is always a way"*** and that one need not accept things the way they are. This attitude would find expressions in significant ways . Secondly, it created a huge sense of dependency within me because my mother took charge of my life in an absolute way. She not only ensured that I prepared but also made up for my mess-ups! That day, unknowingly, I had simply outsourced my life to this gorgeous woman. I guess it's much more convenient to let someone else take charge of your life? What more can one ask for?

There was nothing in the world I feared more than her. I still remember the day I cut my hand. I was a Prefect in school (school leader), but I was also one of its biggest troublemakers! But somehow, because of my academic record, they let me be appointed as one. After becoming the Prefect, I took a bunch of my friends to bunk class. Now we aren't talking about college here but school. Bunking class in school is unheard of. Not surprisingly, it came to be known, and one of my birdies told me that they were planning to strip me off my Prefect position, which was still okay. I didn't care about that. What I did care about is that this news should just not reach my mother. That's it. So I quickly came up with a plan. I recollected seeing some broken pieces of glass on the top floor of my school. I quickly went there and slashed my arms (not wrist) with it until it bled. I then went to the first Aid and got my arms treated. I did all this only so that I could conjure a legit reason for bunking the class!

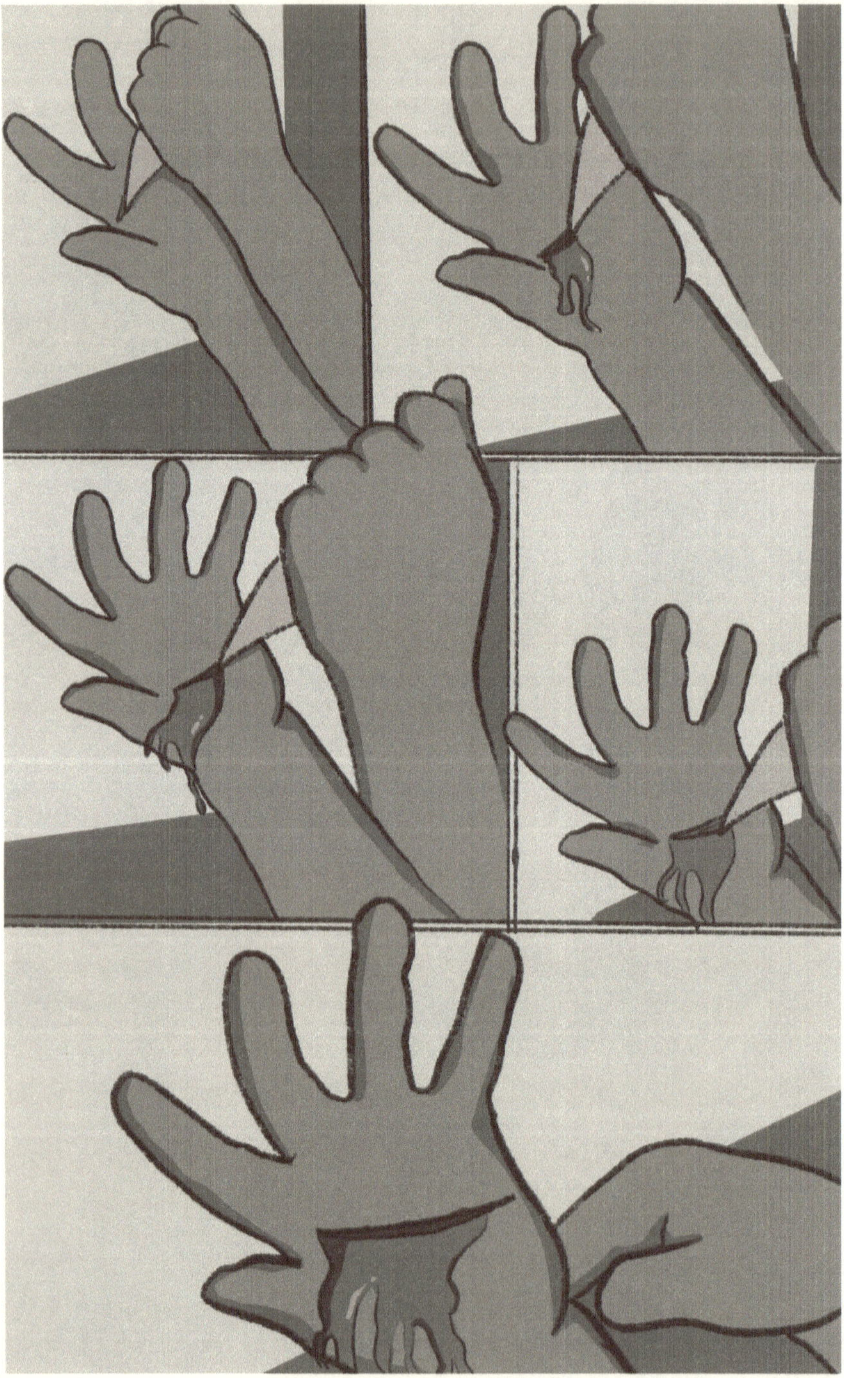

There is also nothing I loved more in life than her. One day, she unleashed her wrath on me for a silly mistake I made in an exam. Now, unlike the West where love is expressed physically, in India, we don't have a culture of hugging and kissing, but that doesn't mean the love goes unexpressed. Indian parents have their own ways, sometimes even by beating! It's difficult to understand, but it's true. So that evening she wanted to get me a Pizza, but Pizza as a food had just entered India in the 90s and wasn't an affordable indulgence for the middle-class. My mother was short of money, so she rang up one of the student's parents requesting an advance from next month's tuition fees. The parent obliged, and I had Pizza for dinner that night. Perhaps the best I ever had!

As I navigated through my dual life in school of academic excellence under my mother's guidance and bank bencher shenanigans, one day as I approached grade 10, something very unusual happened. An occurrence that ever happened only twice and both times it had to do with me. Now, I will tell you about the first time. The incident was that my parents sat together. My mother and father have had a very troubled marriage, to say the least. In fact, growing up, I used to wonder how they even managed to have sex with that kind of friction. Could I have had a virgin birth too, like Jesus? The kind of stuff I have seen as a child, I hope no child has to ever go through! As horrible as a couple they were, they were loving and giving parents, offering their children much more than they could even afford. So suddenly, these 2 sat together and beckoned me. I had to rub my eyes to believe what I was seeing.

"We just wanted to know what your plans are after 10th grade." Without getting into too much detail now, it is sufficient to know that grade 10 is one of life's biggest milestones for an Indian. Even bigger than their marriage! After grade 10, a kid is expected to pick either Science, Commerce, or Arts as his stream of specialisation. The unwritten rule is that the smart kids took science, the average took Commerce, and Art kids are not even humans. Even for my mother to ask me this question was cute because I don't think she fully understood the kind of impact she had on me. Way back in 6th grade, on our way back home from an outing, I casually asked her what I should become in life, and her response was, "You must become an engineer and work for a top company." Her words were like Gospel truth for me. My response was simple, "I want to take Science and then engineering."

"Where do you want to do your engineering from?" they enquired.

I kid you not, I literally knew only one engineering college then. One of the senior guys I used to hang out with, who had a reputation of being a geek, studied there. So, pretending to have done my research, I said, "Sardar Patel Institute of Technology," I said. "Ok then, good luck to you! Let us know anything you want."

In India, there are 2 education systems running parallelly - one, the public schools you go to because you have to, and since they are usually not good enough, you also go to a cram school where you pay exorbitant fees to learn what public schools should be teaching you in the first place. This parallel cram school industry for Engineering entrance exam is a multi-billion-dollar industry, bigger than even Bollywood! Unfortunately, the cram school I wanted to prepare at had closed admissions, but it barely bothered me. I simply let my mother know, and we, of course, know what followed. I ended up getting admission there.

By this time, I had lost interest in academics, and given that my mother was no longer leading my academic effort, I was barely motivated to do well.

My childhood friend Darshan Ashar (yes, the same guy who got reprimanded for simply sitting with me) and I had a pact. The day our results arrived (the final score would be out of 200), we would conceal our marks. We would first reveal the first digit, which had to be 1 as we, the great men of our times, deserved a triple-digit score at least. We would then slowly reveal the second digit, and if it happened to be any less than 8 (meaning, if we scored less than 180), we would simply tear the report card as it wasn't reflective of our true geniuses! When the scores arrived, my friend had scored a glorious 157, and I was just 4 marks behind him with 153. To get into Sardar Patel, a minimum of 180 was needed. Where am I going to study now, what am I going to do now? God knows. And They did.

Soon after my results, my mother, some of her sisters, and my cousins set out on a family outing in the city. We were visiting a few temples, one of which was the Mahalaxmi Temple beautifully located across the expansive Arabian sea. Mahalaxmi is the Goddess of Wealth and Prosperity. I always looked forward to visiting this temple as a child because there was a sugarcane juice vendor on the premises.

For those who haven't had sugarcane juice in their life, I have some interesting ways you could kill yourself. It is also said that one of Parashurama's weapons is secretly concealed in this temple with utmost protection.

Anyway, after paying my respects to the beautiful Goddess and having my glass of pristine sugarcane juice, I came out waiting for the rest of the family. With nothing to do and in the pre-mobile internet era, I called up my friend Karan, who had scored a 154 (he lied; I later found out that it was only 42 or something like that).

A few mins into the call, I ask him how his friend Suman is doing. I had met Suman just a few days ago when I visited Karan's house. The reason I asked about Suman was because he was an unforgettable character - an actual shoplifter. I didn't believe it at first when Karan told me this. I thought they were both playing a silly prank with me. I think Suman felt offended, so in order to clear my doubts, he went into a store and in a few seconds, came out with a handful of CDs! It's a sight I remember so vividly even today.

On enquiring upon Suman on the phone, Karan remarked that he had gotten into DJ Sanghvi, one of the city's top engineering schools! I was shocked because for "some reason" Suman didn't quite seem to be someone who was academically bright. "How?!" I exclaimed to Karan with a mix of shock and surprise. "Oh, he got through NRI (Non-Resident Indian) quota," explained Karan. "What do you mean by NRI quota, he clearly resides in India scamming stores. I've seen it!" I said with ridiculous disbelief. "Haha, yeah, but his father is an NRI," said Karan. "Wait, so is my father," I told him. "Can you give me Suman's number immediately?" I asked to which Karan obliged. I called up Suman, and it turns out the Government of India had introduced a reservation of seats in colleges for "Children of Indian workers abroad." I had missed NRI quota admissions for almost all schools (can't blame me because WHAT THE HECK IS NRI Quota?), but Suman mentioned I could still make it to one school - Sardar Patel Institute of Technology!

So I went to Sardar Patel, my dream college, the very next day. I met the in-charge and told him that I had come for NRI admissions. To double-check, I asked if it was okay that I wasn't an NRI but my father was. "No," he said, "You must be an NRI."

Dejected, I started walking out. Right at the exit, I bumped into an old friend whose marks I knew and was hence surprised to see her there. "What are you doing here?" I asked. "Oh, I came here for NRI admissions," she said. "But that guy in there just told me that I must be an NRI," I said, confused. "Oh, he doesn't know a thing. I've read the guideline fully, just do what I say," she said in words that filled my heart with inexplicable joy.

I did as she said. I got into Sardar freaking Patel Institute of Technology. That's not it. Turns out, it was the first and last time there was an NRI quota in the college. Never before that year, never after!

Everything was going just as planned - whose plan, I don't know but somebody's plan indeed. I was now to become an engineer, take up a job, and be a capitalism-loving, God-apprehensive guy. But remember, everything you can say about me, the opposite is true as well. I would never end up taking a job and, in fact, end up meeting God or Gods, maybe? 😵

Please scan this code to unlock $GIC tokens and
Bonus content for this chapter

Question 3 -

What were those childhood incidents that had a deep impact on you - the good, bad, ugly, and nice! The country you grew up in, school you went to, friends you made, books you read, movies you watched, relationships you had, Everything of significance that touched your life… Whatever comes to your mind…Write it down.

Chapter 04

Ludo

The game doesn't end with the cards you draw.
It ends based on how you play your cards.

Ludo

There was a point in my life just after my first book got published where the only thing I did all day was to play ludo online. I mean, it got so bad that my roomies started to get concerned. You should know that guy roommates are quite a species. I think they should be studied in a lab. They are so indifferent to everything around them that, let's say, even if aliens showed up in their living room, it would go unnoticed or ignored (unless the roomie is Joe Rogan, of course). This actually happened in one of the houses I lived in. There were just so many people moving in and out of the house all the time that this one guy stayed in for so long that everyone just assumed he was a part of the house. It is only later that we realised who he was. This is what transpired: one of the original inhabitants had got his friend to stay for a short time. This friend then got his countryside cousin to stay with him for a short time. The friend left after a while, but the cousin stayed. He watched television shows in his native language, ate home food like a boss. He is the kind of guy who took the phrase "Just treat this as your own house" to another level, so much so that it actually became like his house that others were living in. Then one day, the planets aligned and somehow one of the guys noticed that he had never in fact seen this guy go to work ever. Then, after a little bit of investigation, this guy's identity was known. Protocol was followed. Nobody spoke to the guy directly. The OG inhabitant first dialled his friend, who then asked his cousin to politely leave with a generous notice of 2 days.

So now you know, things must be really bad when even my roommates started noticing that I was only playing ludo all day. Do I regret it? Well, let's just say if I had instead bought 1 or 2 Bitcoins, then instead of playing ludo all day, I WOULD BE THE CHIEF CRYPTO ADVISER TO THE WHITEHOUSE, OK. That too only after they pleaded with me after multiple visits to my secret private beach ranch in Malibu. If future versions of you would reminisce about their earlier versions, it would look like this - The 30s, 40s, and 50s version of you pleading to the 20s version of you to do things differently.

I'll tell you a secret - that's the magic age, OK. The 20s. As far as exploring oneself is concerned - there is no age better than the 20s - it's not that one cannot do it after that - but it becomes increasingly difficult.

20s is literally the age to fuck-up and keep trying so that you don't mess up the rest of your lives. Imagine this - till your teens - you don't have the emotional, mental, financial, or physical bandwidth to explore yourself. In your 30s - you may still have the body (depending on how you treated it in your 20s), emotional maturity, and finance on your side, but your ability to take risks reduces drastically. In your 40s and 50s, body may not be on your side, and unless you've taken conscious efforts, even your mind may not be as sharp as it used to be and with an entire family's burden on your shoulder, the ability to take risks is 0. The next best time is your 60s - no responsibilities, no risks, you have the money but without your peak body or mind and an uncertain amount of life remaining, will it be as fruitful an exploration?

All said and done, coming back to ludo, as much as I wish I had done so much more in my 20s, I did discover one fascinating thing about life in that phase though. I felt among all the games I had played until then, ludo was one game that came very close to life because winning ludo is a factor of 2 things - one is luck because it involves the roll of dice, but that's not it - how you play out your coins determines the other part of your game. You can have the most terrible roll of dice and still win the game or have the best and still lose! The Chapters till here were mainly about my roll of dice - and if you've been filling the diary - your roll of dice too. The genetics, the ancestry, the upbringing, and all the other micro and macro events over which you had little to no control. The phase of life from here on is about how I play the roll of dice. Oh, and I love to play! In many ways, I live to play. For the first time in my life, I started exploring who I am - not wanting to be like anyone - at the same time, I cant's say I was simply being me because I had no clue who I was - an exploration in that direction had just begun and in the process, I make unbridled love, make loads of mistakes, found an award-winning start-up, sell chai, create crowdfunding history, travel extensively, compile a bestselling book, work on its OTT adaptation, and deliver a viral TEDx talk. I know you are perhaps wondering where the other juicy stuff is - meeting God, meeting Parashurama, Crypto etc. That too happened, of course. Let me tell you this - If I hadn't done what I did in my 20s, there is no way God would have ever met me.

With no God or Spirituality anywhere in foresight yet, in my early 20s it would all change that fateful night when I would sleep with a strange book under my pillow. When I woke up, something had happened and life wasn't the same. But how did a guy who just set out to get a degree in engineering and find a job end up in such a position in the first place? Fasten your seatbelt, you may need it from here on! So much to say. Where to start? Of course, from where we ended the last chapter. Sardar Patel Institute of Technology.

Even before I stepped foot on campus, I had managed to become one of the most (in?) famous guys in college. More curiously, almost everyone in my college knew me (and continue to even today) as "Anna," a South Indian moniker for an elder brother or, more colloquially, you can call it an equivalent of "Bro." The association was so strong that even my then-girlfriend called me that. Even in bed! But how did I get there? It's a story that involves a now defunct social media platform, fake profile, ragging, and playing with religion!

There was a time I managed to take revenge on a guy who I doubt even today knows who did that to him. This must have been somewhere around 2006. I think Mark hadn't made Facebook public yet, and it was still exclusively like a Harvard deal. Orkut was then the most popular social media platform in the world - or at least in India. Unlike Facebook where admin details of a page are kept private, on Orkut, "communities," the equivalent of today's Facebook Page, would have its admin detail public so one could actually connect with them if they wanted to. I had then just joined what was the largest community page for my hometown Mumbai in anticipation of sharing my love for the beautiful city I owed so much to. Unfortunately, the community had become a cringy fan page for its admin! Desperate yes-men, who were seeking to be promoted as moderators, would start threads admiring their "beloved" admin who would then reward these sycophants and make them moderators. Supposedly, it was a huge deal for many. What all man does for any sense of social status! Anyway, I openly expressed my displeasure over this nonsense, and the next thing I knew was that I was banned from the community. It enraged my teenage hormones big time. I knew this wouldn't end well. For them. Over the next few hours, I put on my "jholer" hat. This is important. Till date, my jholer hat is one of my most prized possessions. Jhol in Mumbai Hindi refers to "Street smart way of handling things" often in notorious ways, and a jholer is a person who indulges in jhol, i.e., a notorious hustler - even if it requires mending ethics. I scoured over the internet for any information I could find about the admin.

At the end of it, I knew quite a bit about him - his name, what he looked like, where he lived, what he did for a living, etc. Turns out, that he was a young Sikh man, who was conspicuously missing any facial hair, which was surprising because the Sikh religion forbids shaving of facial hair, and such an act is considered blasphemy. I knew exactly what I had to do next. I created a fake profile and pretended to be a Sikh person. Shared this guy's profile across all major Sikh communities urging "my brethren" to stand up for our religion and give this sacrilegious person a piece of our mind. Oh gosh, how easy is a man fooled in the name of God! The next few days, I just sat back and enjoyed the drama. The admin's profile was flooded with threats and abuses. You can say I felt content with what I did. Anyway, as soon as I secured admission into Sardar Patel, the first thing I obviously did was to join its community on Orkut. I initially only observed posts on the page and followed interactions between some of my to-be peers and senior year students. Everything was fun and games until some seniors started expressing their intentions to rag us. Oh boy, Huge mistake! I wasted no time in jumping to action. One of the many things I derive immense pleasure from is what is now known as "Planning & Plotting," which became an internal slang within my friends for my love for strategising and coming up with highly sophisticated plans (often for notorious purposes).

I first removed my DP and changed my name on Orkut to "Anna." Found out a whole lot of information about my seniors and quickly went to the community, sharing everything I knew about them and openly dared them to first find me and then rag me! Without a surprise, the thread had become one of the hottest topics of discussion on campus. It had rubbed my seniors off the wrong way! We were supposed to have a pre-college orientation in a few days, and I told them I was going to be there and wished them luck in finding me. As expected, my seniors swarmed the entrance to the auditorium where the freshman orientation was being conducted like sharks on the prowl! They keenly looked at every student that entered the auditorium with the eye of a hawk!

Obviously, I went back home that day and posted everything in the community. I told them what colour clothes each of them was wearing and where they were standing. I also pointed out that one of them was , in fact, seated right next to me Soon after, college started, and they somehow figured out which class I was in, so they showed up right before the lunch break and barged in.

Of course, I went back home and instigated them once again. I told them how I had managed to escape right beneath their nose by showing some fake receipt to one of them, and they couldn't get me yet again. Tired of this chase, the seniors then suggested that if I was indeed as smart, then I should also be courageous enough to reveal myself. They fixed a time after college hours and also a classroom where I was asked to walk in, where they would be waiting in anticipation. I obliged - I think it was time. I walked into the classroom with at least 15-20 of them. I got ragged. It was friendly, like one would expect of people in Mumbai. Ragging in the northern belt of India can get very ugly though. Anyway, a senior had recorded it all on her Nokia N72, which she would lose months later, so thankfully there is no visual record of the incident anywhere :)

I would go on to develop really close bonds with some of these seniors. Thus, in this dramatic fashion, I commenced one of the most crucial and beautiful phases of my life - A phase where I grew from a boy to a man.

It is in college that I would discover what is easily the sweetest, and one of the strangest relationships a human can have - Friendship. You name any relationship, and I can tell you the underlying transactional dynamics that drive it subconsciously - be it mother-child, boss-employee, mentor-mentee, husband-wife, etc. Every relation has a very animal-like drive to it. We will talk about this in length later, but friendship? I never quite understood this strange bond really. God is shrewd and cunning. Every other bond nature formed is for the sake of its own creation - to keep moving creation forward. God created every relation for their own benefit, but friendship is something humans created themselves. For themselves. It's almost like it wasn't part of the plan! It just happened, and even God couldn't stop it. I cannot emphasise enough how important your friends can be in navigating the course of your life. Remember this, you cannot choose the family you are born into, but you can certainly choose your friend, and within these 2 sets of people, the direction of your life is set in a huge way. My friendships have been one of my life's greatest treasures. Let me introduce you to some of the people I hung out with in college the most -

Pranav-Hrishi

These 2 were like Laurel & Hardy, Tom & Jerry - inseparable and always fighting. They went to the same school, ended up in the same high school, lived in the same neighbourhood, then ended up in the same undergraduate school, in the same class, and it turned out they also shared the same marriage anniversaries!

If AI had to make a caricature of what an average Indian middle-class educated boy would look like, then it would look exactly like Hrishi. He was lanky, spectacled, and oiled his hair with a side partition. I have never seen him change his hairstyle ever in life. It's almost as if it's been like this since birth!

For someone who barely experimented with his hair, you can imagine how he conducted his life. Like a good middle-class boy, after completing his engineering, he went on to secure an MBA degree from a top B-school in India and now works for a top multinational company as a manager.

However, the most distinct part about this guy was that he was always in a hurry. Hrishi never spoke; he rapped. When classes got done, standard scenes between Pranav & Hrishi, who travelled together back home, were like this:

We always wondered how fast Hrishi must be in bed, and that his spouse would get pregnant without them even realising it. Hrishi's child would actually come out in 9 days instead of 9 months! 😄

Pranav was the closest a human could resemble a Panda while still being categorised as human. I kid you not, he literally looked exactly like Kungu-Fu Panda, and he was everything you would expect a person who looks like that to be - cute, affable, endearing, funny, but he was also easily offended (particularly for being called fat), and I derived great pleasure in offending him. This may be difficult to digest, but bullying was such an integral part of going to an Indian school! I feel we live in too sensitive times to even mention the kind of bullying that occurred in my school. So I extended my bullying nature from school to college as well. It is only later in life that Pranav told me how much the bullying affected him and that he had to go through therapy later to overcome it. None of this affected our friendship in any way, though. We literally grew as brothers. I've always had a huge appetite in general for food, particularly for street food. I can relish food from places no dignified human will ever choose to eat at, and yet I would be perfectly alright.

Literally the only other person with whom I shared compassion towards street vendors was Pranav, so eating at the most atrocious street joints became a daily ritual. One day, a friend insisted on joining us, and she had food poisoning for the next 3 days!

Pranav is also one of the intelligent people I have known. I am afraid he would never realise how intelligent he truly is. I have rarely seen people with an ability to grasp things as quickly as he does. Pranav went on to do his Master's at an IVY league college in the US and is now a Software Developer at Google. Of course, his American ass, no longer allows him to relish tacky Indian street food.

With me joining their duo, Pranav, Hrishi & I quickly became a trio. Is it just me, or is everyone literally a part of a close trio of friends? There is always a group of 3 friends! One day, a rather amusing incident happened with the 3 of us. We had gone to the North of India for a college trip, and not surprisingly, the 3 of us were sharing a room. At the time of heading out, Hrishi had (surprisingly) given the room key to me.

This may seem like a scene from a cartoon, but this is exactly what ensued. I was literally the one to lose the key, but nobody told me a thing. Instead, Hrishi and Pranav started arguing in the middle of the lobby, with Pranav blaming Hrishi for giving me the keys! Oh God, how much

I laughed that day. Such was indeed my reputation. It was as if a given that by trusting me with the key was itself the end of it.

Tbh, with my mother around, I never felt the need to grow up, neither did my mother let me. I kid you not, I never even purchased my own underwear until my mid-twenties!

The next close friend I made in college is **Rohit Bhangale**.

Rohit came from a small town called Jalgaon in Maharashtra and is a man of culture. He was the kind of guy for whom Sooraj Barjatya(an Indian filmmaker known to make blockbuster movies with traditional Indian family centric stories and values) made films. In fact, he actually cried while watching *Vivaah*. This is even more commendable given that he comes from a family of great wealth and power. None of us drank or smoked while we were in college, but most of us would do so after graduation. Rohit never had a drink or smoked in his entire life. He never allowed his family's financial security to hamper his academic excellence. He had a terrible fear of public speaking, though. On his first day at SAP Labs, he introduced himself as, "Hi, I am Jalgaon and I am from Rohit."

Rohit & I were so close that on the last day of our college, we were adjudged the best couple in class. , times are such that I must clarify we are both straight and had our respective girlfriends :D But Rohit did behave like my wife, always keeping close tabs on me. Later, we would also end up being roommates during our first jobs in Bangalore. I would often come late as my office was the farthest, and just like an Indian wife, Rohit would be waiting at home, taunting me for coming late, all of this while he watched his favourite TV soap opera!

I don't know if Rohit's wife knows this yet, but while they were dating, I wrote love letters for her on his behest and behalf! He went on to do his Masters in the US and works there as a consultant for one of the Big 4s.

Shruti

Shruti and I started off as best friends, and then this movie called Jaane Tu Ya Jaane Na was released, and we made the mistake of watching it together as a group. The movie revolves around the theme of 2 best friends who go on to discover their hidden love for each other. Well, Mumbai people, you see, we take our movies very seriously, so everybody in the group thought it was their responsibility to get the 2 of us involved, and eventually, we gave in. Shruti was cute, like a penguin; she, in fact, walked like one too. Her father was the CFO for a leading telecom company in India, and an aspect of her I admired the most was how she treated money despite having it in abundance! I used to spend much more than she did, and she always gave me flak for it. Shruti was also one of the major reasons I got through my engineering. I call it God's design. She was just about 5 ft tall. I am 6'2. She was roll no 23, I was 24 and inevitably sat behind her during exams.

Without having to get into details, you know how I cleared. Shruti would cry after every exam, and because I knew her paper better than she did in many ways, I would alert everyone that it was a false cry and that she had performed really well indeed.

Tanush

Tanush, as a popular reference from a Bollywood movie, is one you would call a "Dev Manus" – a "Godly man." Soft-spoken and polite on the outside. He is the kind of guy who would rather keep quiet than talk unnecessarily. In fact, he sailed through the Analytical round for Deloitte, but during the group discussion stage, which can get rather noisy as people spoke for the sake of it, Tanush gave up the offer as he simply couldn't get himself to speak in between the noise! Tanush was an introverted gem that remained hidden from the group for 2 years until I met him, and we bonded over our love for movies and books, and crime stories. Even today, I blindly read a book or watch a movie suggested by him. Tanush also is a complete teetotaller.

Then there were other people like Chinmay who was one of the smartest people around. His excellence was not only academic but 360 degrees. He was a topper, an avant-garde blogger, traded domain names, had won the Star Sports quiz with Harsha Bhogle and rekindled in me a childhood love for Quizzing. Swinburn - The good guy pretending to be bad guy but terribly failing at it. Prashant Ghabak is another dear friend with whom I shared a common love for reading and politics. We also shared a very dark humour and never shied from making fun of our own skin tone(we both were dark-skinned. He much more than me) and showed no mercy in making fun of others on even the most sensitive topics 😎

Like this, in fun and frolic, we appeared for our first semester exams. For Indians, exams closely resemble a war zone. Indians are so triggered by exams that they would prepare vociferously even for those online "Which personality type are you" kind of quiz on the internet. Somehow, I never bothered about exams much. While tense last minute preparations would continue until the moment one enters the exam room, I would be sitting somewhere reading the newspaper.

Watching me, Pranav would come concerned and ask me if there was anything he could teach me last minute. "Haan bhai, please, poora subject padha de," (Yes bro, can you teach me the entire subject please?) would be my response. There would be an awkward silence, and we both would burst out laughing. This was a ritual before every exam 😃

Finally, the day of exam results had arrived. On average, the heartbeat of every Indian student on these days would be around 160s. There is a heightened crowd in temples. God's telephone lines are crashing. The air is filled with nervous breaths, which are palpable. No animal would want to be in the same space filled with eerie tension. Mumbai University was always known to be one of the strictest universities in the country in terms of evaluation. To secure a distinction would mean scoring a minimum of 70%. Typically, across colleges in Mumbai, only 5-10% of students would score this feat. Results were displayed on a notice board. The crowd gathers. I keep away.

Shruti had scored 69%. WTF? WHAT THE FUCK?! I was dating a snake all this while? This girl would freakin come out crying out of exams. She was still crying after the results. It seems it was one of the worst days of her life because she missed scoring a distinction by one mark. Really, woman?

Rohit scored 74%! This bugger, who has to even rehearse his thank you's at the time of presentations and who literally studied with me, got a 74%! BRUTUS ONLY. Bloody backstabber.

Hrishi scored 76%! Now I know what this guy did after teleporting home every day.

Pranav! Omg! How do I say this? This fatso, who I know for a fact, spent more time with me eating street food than studying, scored 83% - eighty fuckin 3! WHAT THE FUCK? Fucking kattappa only.

Chinmay scored 86% ! Looks like all the bloody aliens of Mumbai University are in my group only.

Me? I scored 53% and flunked 2 subjects! 😇

Oh dear. Oh dear. Oh dear, dear me.

While it is true that I didn't care about doing so badly in the exams myself, I just couldn't take the fact that everyone in my group had done so much better than me. 😠 It is a very Asian thing, not many will understand. Your own performance does not matter as much as your friends' performance does 😌. My mother had trained me to become a competitive beast, and oh boy, I always have been one. I was so competitive even as a child that I wouldn't allow my sister to submit entries to Cartoon Network competitions, assuming that they wouldn't accept 2 entries from the same house. So it was only me who submitted entries, and I always won! I have never lost a single contest or election in my life. In fact, one time I won a bumper contest where Cartoon Network had sent Tom & Jerry along with a huge television crew to my house, along with a carton full of goodies! It became quite some news in the neighbourhood.

And here I was with some of the smartest brains in the city, scoring only half as much as them and flunking 2 subjects. I was burning within. With jealousy. With angst. With envy. I was fuming.

I was resolved to make up for this indignation, so I decided to set myself up for bigger academic excellence in the following semester! I feel I had a natural flair for programming and technology, so I took that as the starting point, but it all came crashing down one fateful day. It was a computer programming lab class, and we were given an assignment to complete in JAVA. It was a very basic assignment, so after completing that, I started working on a self-assigned slightly more complicated programme. I wanted to create a hangman game that we backbenchers often played in class, so I immersed myself in the challenge. The teacher comes and notices that I am doing something different. I tried to reason with her that I was indeed programming and, in fact, tackling a more complicated challenge, and that she should, in fact, be happy about it.

My college principal was an absolute boss lady. A forward-looking woman stuck in an orthodox system, doing her best tackling both worlds and did a pretty good job. She was a well-known educationist, dressed gracefully, had short hair, and her daughter studied at Harvard. Fortunately for me, she didn't take any action. But that one incident made a deep impact on me. It created a deep disgust about the education system. And this was 2007, both internet penetration and the overall online education ecosystem barely existed in India, so it's not that I could simply ignore the existing system. I was solely reliant on it. That day I knew I had to make something else of my life. But what? I had to belong somewhere! But where do I belong? What am I supposed to do? How do I find my success? My life until then, I never thought for myself! Neither did I ever question because I didn't even know that was an option! After learning about my result, my mother was honest with me. She told me that I had to figure my way out on my own from here and that she didn't know any better, but my mother had inadvertently shown me a way by doing something very momentous years ago.

When I was around 5 years of age, we had some disposable income at home. Now, the choice in the family was to either spend it on buying this new fancy revolution that was brewing in the world called Computer or to invest in a series of 15 books called Time-Life books that were being sold by a relative of my mother. These books were specifically designed to introduce children to the world by touching upon different topics like countries, science, oceans, wildlife, Dinosaurs, cultures, etc. Each book cost INR 1000, which was a LOT of money for a book in those days. In fact, for a book in these times too! While the rest of the family was looking forward to a computer at home 😎, my mother decided to go for the books. A decision we all resented then, but it turned out to be one of the best decisions she ever made. So at an early age, I developed one of the most significant affairs of my life: my affair with books. Those books made me fall in love with reading and also with the world. They were so beautifully designed, with premium hard-bound, thick paper density that matched its price, so richly coloured that I literally felt teleported with every book I read. I read every book multiple times over! So books and reading, in general, became one of my best friends at a very early age. Unfortunately, the Indian education system does not allow much scope for reading or, for that matter, any life outside academics, so I never quite managed to read a lot of books while I was in school, but I would unfailingly read the newspaper every single day.

Now with an existential crisis confronting me at the age of 17, I knew exactly what to do next and who to resort to. My old friend - Books.

What can I say about a man who makes friends with books? People have an extremely wrong misconception about avid readers. Avid readers don't read books so that they know more. Avid readers read books so that they know how little they know! And this was the first realisation I had when I started reading. How little I knew about this glorious phenomenon called life. Another realisation I had was how little everyone else knew as well! Nobody knew anything, but they just kept going about their life cluelessly! My friends, teachers, family, politicians running the country! This had a major shift on how I looked at life. You can say, in many ways, it is only then, at the age of 17, I truly became a student. Starting afresh. As if I entered this world from another, and it was for me to figure out everything about this strange place. Amongst all the books I read then, there were 2 particular books that had the maximum impact on me. It may not be a coincidence that the themes of these 2 books would also go on to become dominant themes of my life. The first book of those 2 books was Sir Richard Branson's Autobiography titled ***"Losing my Virginity."*** Before you get your thoughts going wild, the book has nothing to do with what you perhaps think it does. Richard Branson is one of the world's most celebrated entrepreneurs and founder of the Virgin group of companies; hence the title. His life is a capitalist fairytale. Born to a mother who was a stripper, he took to entrepreneurship at a very early age. While still in college, he started a student magazine hustling his way through success. Of the few things I remember, he called up Coca-Cola telling them that Pepsi was offering sponsorship to the magazine whereas they weren't, and he would do the same thing with Pepsi, eventually gathering sponsorship from both! Known for his eccentricities, he once set on a hot air balloon, nearly losing his life but then garnering worldwide attention for his stunt. Even more notable was his ridiculous bet on another eccentric and absolutely unknown and troublesome artist called Mike Oldfield. The collaboration turned out to be stuff of legend as the album Tubular Bells became an all-time classic, making Virgin Studios a legendary music label. When I was reading his autobiography, I just didn't want it to end. I remember dreading reaching the end of the book, not being able to handle the void it would create in the next few days.

The second book that made a huge impact has an interesting backstory. There was a business ideating competition that was conducted in college, and all of us had participated in it with great interest. I ended up winning it. I was fresh from reading Richard Branson's book, high on his entrepreneurial journey. You can say it got me a step closer towards realising my own entrepreneurial dream, but at this stage, I still hadn't fully decided to become one. It was not winning the contest itself that made such a big difference in my life as much as one of the guest sessions did. The guest for the session happened to be the dean of a leading B-school in Mumbai (NITIE, which has now become an IIM, and my house in Mumbai is pretty close to an IIM now. How cool is that?) and he opened the session with a strange contest. He said anybody who asked him the first question would receive a book from him about someone who he thought was one of the greatest businessmen in India. The moment I heard Book and Business, I knew I badly wanted this one, but no prizes for guessing who beat me to asking the first question - Hrishi, of course! However, after the session ended, I still went up to the guest speaker and politely asked him if he was carrying more copies of the book and if I could still receive one. He obliged! The book turned out to be the autobiography of Mahatma Gandhi. I found my indulgence for the next few days, and oh man, what an adventure that turned out to be. The book taught me a very important lesson - even the most ordinary men can make something great of their life. India is a very fate-centric country with immense belief in destiny. Most stories involving heroes and Gods have always been of those who were destined to become great, but Gandhi was a guy who flicked pennies off his servant to smoke cheap tobacco. He visited the brothel often with his friends (but did nothing), and when he was supposed to attend to his ailing father, he was so absorbed by his lust that he escaped to the next room to have sex with his wife, and in that span, his father died! This man went on to become one of the most celebrated humans in history! For the first time, I understood, greatness was not something an astrologer predicts at birth; it is something everyone can achieve no matter what they are born into.

Movies became another intimate partner. I watched movies not only as a source of entertainment but as a portal into the world. I miss those days when the world had the fortune of immersing themselves into a 3-hour classic without having to check the phone even once. It bred a different kind of people. A genre I enjoyed watching the most was Psychological Thrillers - Fight Club, Shutter Island, Memento, Sixth Sense, Uff! the one where you realise it was all in the mind?

When all of this was happening, another major world event took place, and it acquainted me with this charismatic guy in the US who launched a revolutionary new phone that would change the face of technology forever. I am, of course, talking about Steve Jobs and the first iPhone. That moment, in many ways, was the final call for me. I just knew at that point where I wanted to belong. I knew I would be launching my own business soon. But this is better said than done. We are talking about India in 2007. There was virtually no culture of entrepreneurship in the country. I am not exaggerating, but hardly anyone even in the country knew what the word entrepreneur meant! The poster boys for Indian entrepreneurship, Flipkart, were just founded the same year with its founder personally selling books door-to-door, and it would take years for them to become a household name. So I was venturing into something that had no precedence in my friends, family, or, for that matter, even my country! Now what business would I be starting? That moment came in a rather interesting manner.

There was a quiz on Gandhi being conducted on campus on the occasion of his birth anniversary. I was, of course, going to participate in it. As preparation, I started to read his autobiography again. There was a professor who had newly joined the college, and there was a lot of fear surrounding his reputation. and how he was infamous for flunking students out of personal vendetta. His name was Nimkar. Why would anyone want to study in such a fearful atmosphere? Attendance was compulsory, so I had to attend his lecture, but instead of wasting my time, I decided to secretly read the autobiography in preparation for the quiz. I was caught and immediately expelled from attending his class. Much later, the professor did indeed live up to his reputation and also failed me in his subject. I ended up coming second in that quiz though. Anyway, there was one good thing that came out as a result of being thrown out which far outweighed the damage of flunking. I got my start-up idea!

There was a habit I cultivated since entering college. I relieved my mother of one activity - picking my wardrobe. I became very particular about what I wanted to wear. Not in a very evolved way and nuanced way, but it was the start of a process. I won't say I had zeroed in on a particular aesthetic, style, or fabric per se, but I started having clarity on what I didn't like. For instance, I was very clear I wouldn't want a single word on my t-shirt that didn't connect with me. I never really understood why someone made and wore t-shirts with random things written on them. One thing I found most ridiculous was t-shirts that had "Since 1927" or "Est. in 2000" printed on them. It really became a huge mystery! I mean, it still made sense why the makers made those t-shirts. Because they were self-absorbed. Because their brand was established in a certain year, it mattered to them, and for whatever reason, they assumed it should matter to others as well! But I still don't understand the decision-making process of someone who goes to a store, then goes through a variety of options, and then picks a t-shirt that has "Est. 2000" written on it, pays to purchase it, and then openly flaunts it as well!

My wardrobe collection carried a lot of kurtas (an Indian style), but it also had a sizeable t-shirt collection, most of which would come from one single brand - it was an iconic brand of those times, now slipped into oblivion. The brand is called Tantra! While very common these days, Tantra was literally the only brand that sold t-shirts with quirky quotes on them. Its designs were funky, witty, sometimes rebellious, and I enjoyed wearing them. It's funny I still remember some of the Tantra t-shirts I owned. I actually managed to pull up some of the ones I wore from the internet for you.

Look closely! ☺

Much to the chagrin of my family and girlfriend, I hadn't shaved or cut my hair for an entire year. As a result, I wore this ☺,

Wore this out of my then well-established admiration for Gandhi

So, in that moment, after being thrown out of that class, I found an innovative way to vent my angst against the system. I found just the perfect way to express myself, and I knew there were many others who would share my frustration. Thus was born Annanymous, a wordplay on Anna and Annanymous.

Now, of course, I knew nothing about making t-shirts, but I knew who to go to. My uncle, who is like a father figure to me and my sister and who also lives with us (after being separated from his wife and has no kids), worked closely in the fashion industry as an advertising guy. He connected me with his friend who manufactured t-shirts. I took Shruti along, and we met the friend at a cafe and understood in detail how a t-shirt is made. For the initial batch of t-shirts, we decided to go with around 4-5 designs and a total of 200 units overall. Now, where will the money come from? Well, one way to look at it is that I am a terrific sales guy, and that comes from my ability to talk and connect with people, but I always feel people are kind to me. Truth be told, nobody has ever denied me anything. If I want something, I simply ask and have it. That's it. It is only much later in "that phase" of my life of which I refer to in

Chapter 01, of which you will learn in detail in Volume 2 , I was denied for the first time ever, but otherwise, I have always received. Naturally, I went to all my friends first, and at the start, there were 10 who on average put around 5K each as investment, and together, we had the ball rolling.

Now, the time had come to design the t-shirts, and for me, that was the easiest part - it came naturally to me. Sam Altman the CEO of OpenAI said something beautiful and wise once in his career advice to someone - he urged them to identify that 'which comes easy to them but hard to other people" . We all have many such skills that baffle others but somehow doesn't seem like a big deal to us and for me Creativity happens to be one of them. You can access the bonus content page to check the designs we created!

The t-shirts were actually supposed to arrive early September, but for some reason, it got delayed and arrived in the evening of September 14th, so the next day was to be our not so grand launch! I am not a huge fan of unnecessary pomp, so I simply arrived in college with a bunch of t-shirts and started selling them. One of the guys who purchased our t-shirt congratulated me on the smart marketing move of launching it on 15th September. Confused, I enquired why he said so. Turns out - it happened to be engineers' day that day! What sweet timing! It didn't surprise me that the t-shirt became a smash hit on campus. I have a good sense for these things, so I knew. Slowly, it spread across the city, and one classmate of mine showed me a Facebook share of his friend from Delhi, and I had no clue my t-shirt designs were going viral nationally! We did not make a lot of money, mostly because every money that we were making, we were putting it back into the business, and also I wasn't the most financially sound person. However, the start-up did earn me numerous accolades. For my efforts, I was listed as one of India's top 30 student entrepreneurs by the NEN at the age of 19. I was either on the front page or full page across most national dailies. The Wall Street

Journal's Mint did a full two-page spread on us, incidentally on the same day when Osama Bin Laden's death covered most full pages across the world.

City students 'bell' varsity cat with slogan protest

K.A. DODHIYA

MUMBAI

Aug. 11: Having had enough of the University of Mumbai's mismanagement of the education system, the final year engineering students of a Mumbai college in the eastern suburbs have come up with a novel protest called "Ghantagiri" involving slogans on t-shirts. According to the students who thought of the concept, it is aimed at ridiculing the education system being followed by the University as well as highlighting the futility of becoming engineers.

The movement has gained momentum and now has a pan-India appeal, with students from other cities also ordering the t-shirts. One of their slogans is "Food, clothing, shelter and 40", where 40 represents the minimum marks students try to get regardless of whether they learn anything or not.

"We thought of many slogans based on popular lines used by protestors and tweaked them to reflect our aims. One of the first slogans we came up with was 'Me (in Marathi script) *ghanta* (depicted by a picture of a bell) engineer'. It means that after graduating we are worthless engineers," said Adithya Iyer, a final year student.

"We have got orders for t-shirts from students of

One of the designs

Pune University and IIT-Delhi after we put the designs on the Internet," said Adithya.

MU senate member Dilip Karande said, "Students have a right to protest but they should speak to the MU vice-chancellor Dr Rajan Velukar rather than resorting to such methods of protest."

This clip is from the front page of Asian Age. This particular design had become almost like a satirical national symbol of angst against the education system. Many businesses would then blatantly rip this particular design and make a huge business out of it. Perhaps even today!

NDTV did a full 10-minute story on us, so I was also on National TV. I was the most famous guy in college, and it earned me a lot of attention from different parts of the country as well. All of this really pleased my parents, and they embraced me for who I am. From wanting me to become like somebody else, they became 2 of my biggest cheerleaders. In a lot of my talks, a recurring question that pops up from students is "How should one convince their parents to permit them to do unconventional things." The answer is simple. I don't think any parent is against their child's best interest - just that parents are stuck with old ideas. Communicating clearly what you intend to do and why or even better by showcasing - with an award, recognition or even a dinner outing sponsored by the first money you make will do the trick. If it doesn't, you go and do what you ought to anyway!

People also don't see the not so glamorous work it takes behind the glamorous celebration. One of my juniors was so enamoured by my achievements that he desperately pleaded to intern with me, so I took him along and he never returned. My usual day at work would be getting into multiple phone calls. One set of calls with my retail customers who would want to place an order for themselves and their friends. There was no e-commerce in India those days. All my business was done on call - not even WhatsApp! Then I would also have various colleges as my B2B clients. It was mainly IIT-Bombay - they had over 14 hostels, and every hostel had around 70-100 residents who would make hostel t-shirts every year, so I would custom make bulk t-shirts for them too. Once I received the order, I would have to call my t-shirt vendor with the details of the sizes of t-shirts I needed. Then I would get into a separate call with my printer whom I had to take through the specific details of the design. First, a sample would be printed, approved, and once the orders were finally ready, I would take the darling Mumbai local train where if I were lucky I would get to sit, otherwise I thoroughly enjoyed, as I now realise, rather perilously, stood at the edge of the compartment, cruising through the sometimes filthy air of the city. The train journey would take roughly an hour one way. My vendors were in this extremely crowded market in Mumbai called Masjid Bunder. It resembled a crowded Arab market in many ways with its multitude of fragrance and an ocean of humans fighting to survive in this decorated chaos. I used to physically carry a bundle of clothes weighing around 5-15 kgs depending on the number of t-shirts, go back the same train for an hour, personally deliver the t-shirts to my retail customers or the hostel, collect the payment for it and then pay my vendors. I was the salesman, operations man, delivery man, finance man, spokesperson and anything else that the business needed me to be.

In case you are wondering how I was running around conducting my business and whatever happened to my college? Well, because my college too ended up earning so many accolades, my principal and Head of Department, Godbole Sir, a very gentle being, were very generous and practical people They knew I wouldn't be up to much academically, but I was doing great for myself and the college in different ways, so my poor attendance was pardoned! Even during my final year project viva, which is supposed to be the grand culmination of my 4 years of studies, revolved around my start-up and not the project itself, much to the surprise of my other 2 project mates 😊 Like I said, people have always been kind! .

Placements had begun, and I opted out of it. I was clear I didn't want to take up a job because by then I knew how society operated. I didn't have to get into something to realise what a scam it is. What happened with engineering was enough! I was the head of every student body that there was, including the placement cell. As part of my customary interaction with a particular hiring lead who came to campus, I mentioned to him about my start-up over a casual chat. He was kind enough to offer me a job even though I hadn't applied! I politely declined. Half of my friends were placed in the top 10% salary bracket. Some of my female friends had been placed in Deloitte, and they were aware that they would either be asked to report to Mumbai or Hyderabad. Mumbai people have a huge resistance towards moving out of the city, and my friends would rather not take up the job than move to Hyderabad. So, I created a fake email ID pretending to be an HR from Deloitte and sent all of them an email about the details of their reporting to Hyderabad. Chaos ensued; one of them started crying. Multiple calls were made to their families informing them of this grave injustice. I watched all this drama with great pleasure. Then they decided to call Deloitte and insist on a change of location, and only then broke out the news to them 😄

The other half of my friends were anxiously waiting to hear from their dream universities in the US. I knew Pranav and another friend called Swinburn were desperate to go to Cornell. I created a fake ID from Cornell and rejected both their applications. They believed. After I revealed the prank, my friends felt I went too far with this one, but to be honest, it would have been much worse had I accepted their application and raised their expectations. Both of them eventually did end up graduating from Cornell.

Tanush and I had created a tradition of making farewell movies for our senior batches. They were smash hits. When it came to our own farewell, we wanted to do it ourselves. Joined by Rohit, we spent the last two weeks or so planning, shooting and editing a roughly 100- minute video, in which we dedicated 2-3 minutes caricaturing each member of our class. There were bursts of laughter throughout. For the visuals towards the end, I had chosen this particular song titled *Yaadein(Memories)* from a Pakistani band called Roxen. Almost nobody wanted the video to end. Nobody wanted college life to end. The HoD was present at the time of screening too. He cried. Others wept.

Shruti and I headed back home together, as we did every day of our lives for the last 4 years. Only this would be the last time we did so. There was prolonged silence for the first 15 mins of the ride; none of us spoke, and then we both burst out weeping at the same time in a way both never had in 21 years of lives.

While I am thankful to Annanymous for so many things, I am utmost grateful for the realisation it brought into me at that tender age of 19. After Annanymous, Fame & Money no longer mattered to me as much as it did until then. But the pursuit of it gave me the joyous thrill but once I had it, It left me with a haunting void and a deep desire to fill that void and hence in a move that may have shocked a lot of people, I decided to shut it down at the end of my campus life. I asked myself a simple question, if the world has one t-shirt company less, what difference would it make? Zilch. Nothing. So, it made no difference to me as well. And I am so thankful for all of that happening so early in my life, else I would have spent a large chunk of my life simply chasing those 2 things. I didn't want to do something just for the sake of doing it. It had to mean something to me and for that, it also had to mean something to the world. What would it be? Because I knew only the Capitalist way, it had to be a more meaningful business idea. What would that be? I didn't know.

After college, for roughly 3 months, I was at home. Just as a side hustle, I still continued servicing hostel orders at IIT-Bombay. I really owe that college. There was slight pressure from the family to find a job, but at the same time, they were happy to have me at home after long as I barely spent any time at home during 4 years of college. Then one day, while reading the newspaper, a headline struck me like a bolt. It zapped me and in just a few seconds of calculation, I knew what my next move was going to be.

The article read *"Harvard Grad sells chai in Bangalore."* There were just so many pointers in that headline itself that made me want to join the endeavour. First, Harvard grad - I knew the importance of the right boss early in your career is much more significant than the job itself. Somewhere in my Planning & Plotting, I kept an MBA from an IVY league college as my Plan B and a recommendation from him would really help. Second, chai - I loved the simplicity of it! Chai is an integral morning ritual across most households in India. In fact, it is the second most consumed beverage after water. Fantastic business! Third, Bangalore - Rohit and Tanush were both in Bangalore for their job in SAP Labs so I got to join them. Joining the start-up wasn't quite the next move I was looking for - but it was just the right pit-stop until I found my next big meaningful start-up idea. I thought this would be a fantastic learning experience. Remember how my mother spoke her way through allowing me to re-appear for the question I had missed in school exams? From that experience, I knew I had the confidence to talk my way through anything I wanted, and I did exactly that. I hounded Amuleek, the founder, into letting me join the small team that included guys senior to me who had graduated from some of the top universities in India (IITs & IIMs mainly). The average age of the team was 30. At 21, I was to become their youngest member.

While I was preparing to leave for Bangalore, a beautiful incident happened. Javed bhai, my t-shirt printer, kept calling me repeatedly. I knew why he was doing so. One of my last orders at IIT, the girls' hostel who I had delivered t-shirts to, didn't pay me so as a result I couldn't pay Javed bhai. As evident from his name, Javed bhai is a Muslim, but he knew the dates of every Hindu festival more than I did because those would be the peak season for him to print t-shirts. So I kept ignoring Javed bhai's calls, but one day it got frantic so I had to answer. Before I could say anything, he broke out "Adhitya bhai, woh main paise ke liye call nahi kar raha tha, meri shaadi ho rahi hai toh uske liye aapko invite bhejna a tha."(Adhitya bro, I am not calling you for the unpaid invoice but to invite you to my wedding!)

That's Mumbai for you! With that, for the first time, I was to leave this darling city and move to another - one with which I would form a deep connection - and maybe that's where I met Parashuram? And another mysterious lady!

There is perhaps no city in the world where there is such a rich mix of the modern and traditional blending so gloriously. Bangalore is one of the epicentres of the profound and ancient art of Carnatic music, and it is also the rock capital of the country. In the traditional part of the city, one of the most endearing sights is the early morning gathering of friends over what is easily the best coffee in the world - Filter Coffee.

But Bangalore is also the beer capital of India. There is the traditional mainland of Jayanagar, Malleshwaram, Basvanagudi - the city's cultural capital where one finds Indian mothers elegantly draped in South Indian Saree playing MS Subhalakshmi's Suprabatham early in the morning. On the other end, there is the modern chaos of the cosmopolitan Whitefield, home to some of the biggest corporate houses from all over the world.

Incidentally, my first day of the job happened to be the day Steve Jobs died. So my friends and I, in tribute to the genius, purchased black turtlenecks and wore them to our jobs

Reading Steve Jobs' Autobiography in the divinely pleasant weather of Bangalore remains one of my most cherished book experiences. One particular thing that stood out for me from his life was his spiritual sojourn to India where, amongst other things, he learnt the art of orgasming without ejaculation. This seemingly strange practice was one of the reasons jobs' then-girlfriend split with him. My stint at Chai Point was pretty nondescript yet very significant in getting me a step closer towards finding my purpose in life. Let's just say my then boss' leadership left me asking for more. For some reason, even with a small team of 5, he never made me feel included - there was always this distance he maintained as one would expect in a full grown corporate structure and not a fledgling start-up. . I could see an almost sickly obsession with fancy degrees in him quite conspicuously - I could see when he introduced the team - what was that one thing about everyone he mentioned first - of all the wonderful things, he always chose the degree first!. I think he also housed a certain complex because he was from Harvard and all his batch mates must be top-notch hedge fund managers, or leading cutting-edge tech companies in the world whereas all he was doing was selling chai. So I could sense a superficial urge in him to make things look fancier than they actually were, ruining the simplicity of the product. For instance, he convened an important meeting once, and he wanted us to go all in on a fancy-sounding Earth-something initiative. It was one of those sustainability initiatives. I found it quite ridiculous for a 1-year-old company teething with many core problems to even bother about. But I knew where it was coming from. Amuleek was like a child. I think what he looked forward to the most was flaunting to his Harvard group. All this Sustainability, Green Earth initiative frills nobody cared about in India in 2011. It seemed like a cool thing to flaunt to his Harvard friends in America. So he did it. But the final nail in the coffin for me was that one meeting. The meeting revolved around a certain "UTF" that the company was launching. The way Amuleek was talking about it in the meeting, it seemed like a very important thing, almost like a Nuclear Weapon. . I had no clue what UTF meant and didn't want to appear dumb in front of these guys, so I pretended to understand what it meant. But soon after the meeting was over, I asked a colleague of mine with whom I was close as to what UTF really meant.

"Use & Throw Flask," came his stunning response. Sane people would call it a disposable flask or just well, a Use & Throw Flask? After that meeting, I dropped any plans of going to Harvard or doing an MBA. I don't mean to generalise, but I feel an MBA is too much faff and has too little substance. But it's not that I didn't learn anything from Chai Point. I learnt quite a lot.

Whether or not the boss behaved like a leader, he certainly looked like one, and that's what I admired most about him. He was impeccably dressed with a neatly trimmed beard and gracefully draped turban. Because this was my first-ever job, I had absolutely no clue what goes on in corporate. I would come to the office wearing shabby kurtas, and one day Amuleek explained to me the importance of dressing well, particularly in a sales job.

One of my later managers, Tejus, who was then CFO of the company, while giving me my first job review, said something interesting. We were in his car, crossing the famous Chinnaswamy cricket stadium when he told me there are 2 kinds of people in the world. One like Virender Sehwag and the other like Rahul Dravid. For those unaware, both batsmen are Cricketing greats with totally contrasting styles of playing the game. Rahul Dravid was nicknamed Mr Dependable for his conservative, traditional, and disciplined approach to the game. Virender Sehwag, on the other end of the spectrum, was known for his maverick style of playing, often going for the big risky shots even on the most unlikely of occasions. Tejus told me that people like Sehwag are born with a gift and rely solely on it, and it could often lead to performances that were flukes. Rahul Dravid, on the other hand, was more process and discipline oriented, which meant that he may have been less flamboyant but much more consistent in his performances than Sehwag was. Well, the basic premise of what he was trying to say is that relying solely on your talent and skills, no matter how abundant, may not be sufficient and that one needs to cultivate the right attitude and discipline to consistently do well. Although I really admired Tejus for his advice then and still do, I would take it with a pinch of salt today. As I would advise you to take anybody's advice - including mine. This is because everyone comes with their unique *Swadharma* and it is silly to expect everyone to harbour similar traits, attributes, characteristics, or attitudes. I am glad that Sehwag didn't follow Rahul's footsteps and vice versa, and eventually, we got 2 unique individuals - different from each other - playing their respective roles well.

Not to dismiss the suggestion that I needed to work on myself. Who in their 20s doesn't think they are infallible? Of course, I thought I was perfect and too arrogant to look at myself with even an iota of criticism. Another piece of advice that stayed with me was the one I received from another colleague who was a consultant at Bain & Company prior to joining the team, that no matter what work you do, your job is essentially to make your boss' life easier. Now that I work with a team, I can vouch for this too. And if you escalate it further up - your goal should be to make God's life easier - perhaps this is the origin of the saying "God Helps Those Who Help Themselves?" - But the ultimate learning from Chai Point came from my sales job early in my two-year stint. As part of my role, I had to go from office to office pitching ourselves as their new chai vendors.

I strongly believe every person should do sales at some point in their lives because it teaches a very important skill: the art of handling rejection.

Two realisations beautifully dawned on me at the same time. On one hand, I realised there isn't much to learn or grow for me at Chai Point anymore, and I started looking for the next thing to do - something more meaningful that would add value to my life and that of others. The answer was right in front of me. Literally. When I used to be at the stores, selling chai and talking to customers, most of them would inevitably turn out to be frustrated engineers. I dug up some numbers and found out that in Bangalore, 1 in 20 IT employees contemplates suicide in life. I knew by then the importance of a great story and had a knack to identify and tell them. I would much later come to know, and so will you, that this is perhaps one of the most powerful skills a person can ever have, across time - storytelling. I knew the story of Indian engineers was one desperately waiting to be told.

To ascertain if the story really is as big as I thought it to be, I set on a pilot trip to do some first-hand research. Remember the friend Darshan Ashar - who got picked up by the teacher in class for sitting next to me? He later went on to do his Masters in the US and settled there. I explained to him what I was doing and why, and that I sought his kind support in sponsoring the pilot trip. "Bank Details Please!" came his swift response, and with that generous mail, I commenced on the pilot trip.

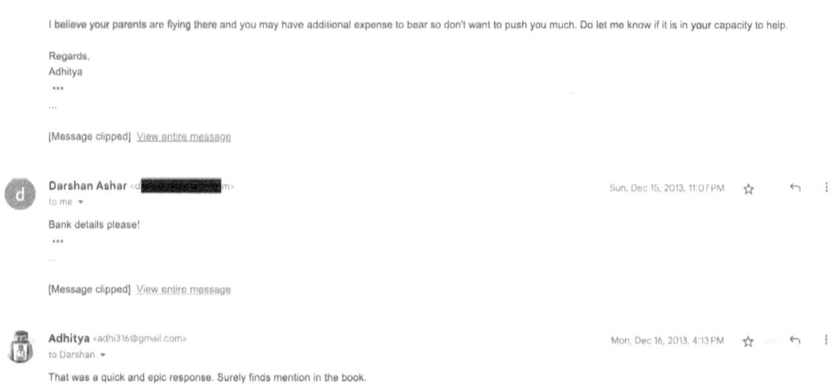

That's why I said friendship is strange. First, you remain friends with the person who gets you in trouble and then also give him money when he asks for it. Now, was the story of India's Engineers as big as I thought it would be? Not at all. It was MUCH bigger. I knew this book would do well and it deserved more attention and resources from me than I had initially anticipated. I was then doing random gigs to sustain myself - one of which was to play the role of an extra in a low-budget movie by a seemingly non-descript debutante director. I would later learn from the Papers one day that it had become India's official entry to the Oscars. While all of this was happening, someone mentioned this site called Kickstarter to me, which was the world's biggest crowdfunding platform, and a lot of creative people went there to seek funds for their project. I had no clue such a thing existed in the world before that day. That's the beauty about capitalism; if you are in need of something, chances are good that some guy somewhere has already solved that problem. When I looked up on Kickstarter, I was blown away. Firstly, crowdfunding means nothing but a sophisticated form of begging. Secondly, Kickstarter was not just a platform but a brand in itself. Projects funded on Kickstarter have ended up attaining cult status over the years, and some of them have even gone on to win an Oscar! I knew I wanted the "Funded by Kickstarter" tag on my book somehow. It really mattered to me, but there was a problem. Kickstarter wasn't available to Indian creators then, and crowdfunding as a concept itself was alien in India, leave alone there being native Indian crowdfunding platforms. It was time to put on my jholer hat once again - There is always a way and you just need to figure it - and I did - jhol discovered. Among the countries Kickstarter was available in was Australia. One of my school friends Kapil, who we used to call Kancha because he was Nepali (I told you we Indians are casual racists 😊), Kancha had moved to Australia after school and become a citizen there. I explained to him my Planning & Plotting, and he graciously agreed to offer his name to the campaign as a proxy for my campaign. So even now if you see, my Kickstarter campaign is under a certain "Kapil Sharma's" name. Now, here's the thing about Kickstarter - it's an all or none game. Which means, you select an amount you want to raise and the number of days you want to raise that amount in. You either raise the full amount in that time frame or you get nothing.

In our case, we had set a target of roughly $14,000 to be raised in 30 days, which means even if we manage to raise only $13,999, Kickstarter would refund all the backers, and we would get nothing. So we took up the challenge. The first thing, we got off to a fabulous start. Kickstarter had picked us as a part of their exclusive "Staff Pick" projects. Staff Pick projects are those that the folks at Kickstarter personally like and endorse. They have a much higher chance of meeting their goal. We were elated but got nowhere 😃 As you can see below, with just 3 days to go, we had not even raised half of our goal.

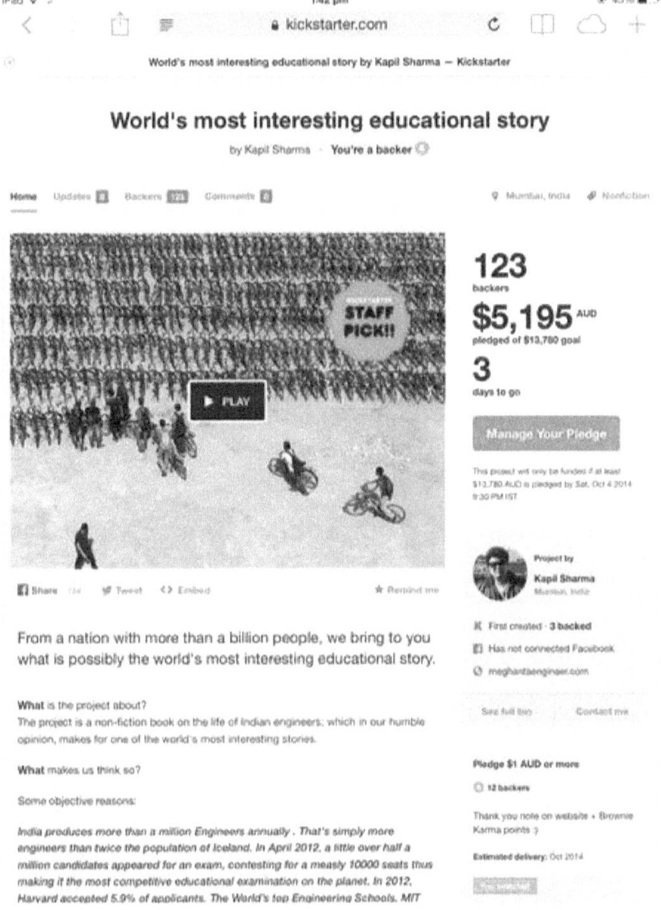

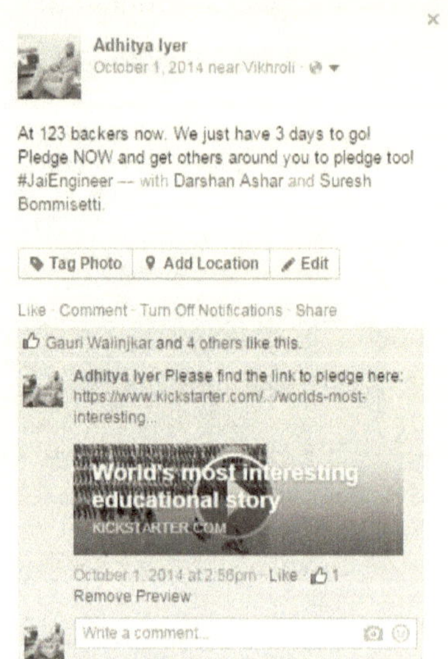

The problem was that nobody in India knew what crowdsourcing was, so we first had to explain it to them and then ask for money. Also, because the community on Kickstarter was mainly western and our story was primarily Indian, none of them seemed to be interested in backing us despite being a Staff Pick. It had indeed drained all of us on the team. It was all very frustrating. With just 3 days to go, it seemed like we were in for a lost cause - then I received a notification that would change the game in a big way.

One of my elder cousin brothers, Prasad Anna, who is based out of Dubai and had become like a poster boy of success within the family, had been closely monitoring the campaign and had made a massively generous contribution - I think around $3,000 or so - and almost overnight, our campaign had crossed 50% of our goal. My parents cumulatively had over 12 siblings, and we all grew up as a close-knit family in sync with the Indian tradition. This is when I realised how crucial the Indian Family value system is in maintaining its unique social structure. It's one of India's biggest strengths over any other culture in the world.

So what next? You know, there is no community in the world that works as slowly as an Indian Engineer days before a deadline, and there is no community in the world that works as fast as them as the deadline approaches. The campaign soon became a fiesta. Everyone wanted it to succeed. There was a strange thrill. Like Gamification. People started reaching out to their friends - and then those to theirs. It was crazy! In a dramatic, nail-biting turned finger-biting finish that went on until the very last minute, we successfully managed to raise our target, and we were now a project "Funded by Kickstarter" 😎

Over the next few months, I set on a journey that would baffle me, fascinate me, depress me, become a cause of great disillusionment, and after all the turmoil, leave me right at the doorstep of my purpose in life. It was the first time I set foot out of Mumbai to travel alone, and I realised why my friends in Mumbai were so reluctant to move outside the city because Mumbai is indeed very different from the rest of the country. During one of my trips, I came across a place in the city of Kanpur which was named Kakadeo but came to be called "Coaching *Mandi*" or "Coaching Market" referring to it being the hub for students who wanted to be coached into cracking the various Engineering entrance exams. I got talking to the local *Paanwaalah(a betel leaf vendor)*, who along with *Rickshawalas (local tuk tuk drivers)*, are always privy to the hottest gossip in town. So I ask this dude, how did this place come to be the way it is. He said a certain Juneja sir had started teaching here first and given his success, other teachers thronged to the place as well, and it gradually became the hub it is known to be today. I went on to ask him where can I meet this Juneja sir's son who supposedly took over the reins from his dad. In a moment that is so vivid to me even today, he first spat the tobacco in his mouth, laughed and told me "Sir, woh to upar hi milenge unka murder ho chuka hai."(Sir, you can only find him up there now because he was murdered) I didn't know what to say. I quickly went back to my room to Google if he was indeed speaking the truth. Turns out not only was he right, but it seems another professor who taught Chemistry showed up at his classroom, like every morning. But this time, 2 gunmen came on a bike and shot him dead in a chilling daylight murder. Two shots to the chest and one to his head. He died on the spot. I am sure my Kickstarter backers wanted me to stay alive at least until the book they financed got published, so I ran out of the place with no regard for time or space.

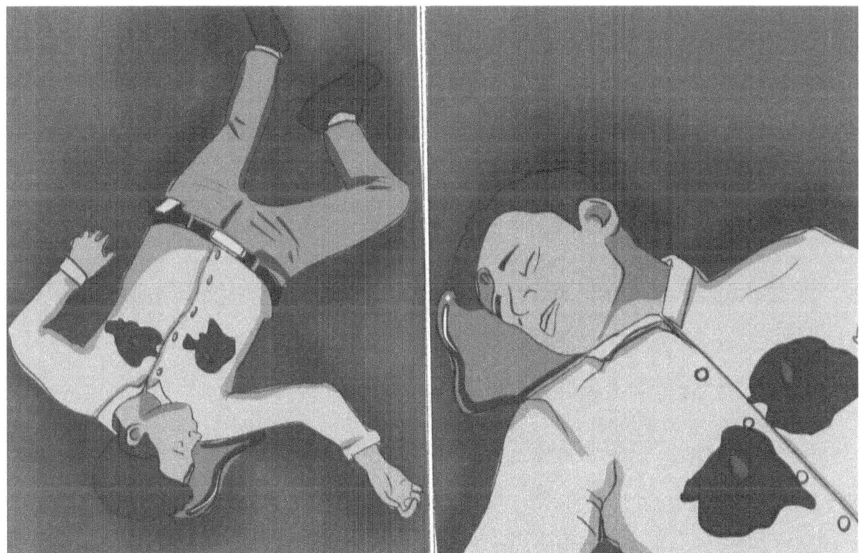

But what depressed me the most was my findings about the state of schools in India. Suddenly, my resentment about the education I received turned into gratitude. I realised that the education I received was, in fact, that of the top 3% in the country because the rest of the country was indeed in a tragic condition. Around 25% of teachers in India were absent on any given day and amongst those present in classes, only half of them chose to teach. The remaining half were either cutting vegetables in class, playing Candy Crush, or sending students to purchase alcohol or tobacco for them! I realised, just by being born to the parents I did, I managed to receive the education I did. But my biggest discovery was one of the most sinister discoveries of my life and of yours too. Now, from here on I want YOU to wake up and read, okay - not your role but YOU. Before I proceed, remember I promised you to reveal the magic trick from the second chapter here? So, here we go.

The trick was complete even before you realised. Everything was done and dusted in those initial few steps only. If you do the math right, then no matter what number you pick, the final answer will always be 4.

What about from there? Everything after that was just an illusion and you didn't have much of a choice, really. I gave you only an illusion of choice. The most common country one can think of from D is always Denmark. The most common animal is inevitably Elephant. So all I had to do was exploit your predictability. Feel cheated? You better do, because something far worse has happened to you.

Whether or not you went to school in India or elsewhere, you have been deceived. Our schooling system was designed to make donkeys of people and it did an excellent job.

Sugata Mitra, the winner of TED prize in 2013, explains the gut-wrenching origin of our schools. "The schooling system as it is today goes back to 400 years of an empire's colonisation and this empire needed 3 kinds of people: Soldiers to protect their land interest; clerks to run their offices and, after the industrial revolution; assembly line workers to make things. So for 400 years we produced millions and millions of people like them and what are the properties of those people? They should be able to understand instructions, follow them and most importantly, they should not ask questions and they should not be creative. Imagine if an assembly line worker started being creative!" To produce millions of such people, what the empire basically needed was a system that kind of worked like a factory. You take raw materials, subject all of them to exactly the same processes and conditions and finally test them. The finished products that clear the test are ready to be sold and the remaining products are simply passed off as defects. The empire managed to build such a system and a very efficient one that: The schooling system. Our childhood has been very deceitful. We are all essentially products of a huge factory. But slowly and surely, a lot of things about our schools begin to make perfect sense after this discovery. Pointers below are by no means a co- incidence:

Chatham Is
Falkland Is
The empire is vast!
BRITISH EMPIRE
But we need more...
Soldiers
Factory workers
Clerks
Administrators
Sir!
This batch is going to pass with flying colors!
MASS PRODN.
PASS FAIL!
BATCH!
EUREKA!

TRRRNNYY'
HOOOOOOO
SCIENCE
MATHS
HINDI
ENGLISH
SST
PRINCIPAL
FAIL
PASS
PASS OUT
BATCH 26 AC.
BATCH of 2009

Both illustrations above from my first book The Great Indian Obsession: The Untold Story of India's Engineers.

Batch: Ever wondered why we are all addressed as a batch? We call ourselves the batch of 2011 or the batch of 1950 and sometimes even take great pride in belonging to these batches. That's how they address sorted and tested products in factories: Pack them in neat boxes and call them a batch.

Bell: Remember the good old bell ringing in school? In a factory, the bell rings to signify a change of shift or lunchtime.

Grouping: Kids are enrolled in school and are expected to progress based on the year they were born in, not based on their level of learning, just like products progress in an assembly line.

Teachers: The role of teachers in schools is exactly that of instructors in factories. They are meant to pass on information and ensure it is being followed.

Testing: Products are tested in a factory and are stamped "Pass/ Ok" or "Fail/Defect" based on which they are either sold or discarded, respectively. The point of testing in school is not to check your learning levels and strengths, but to certify you as useful or useless. So, for some reason, if you have a tough time remembering when Shah Jahan was born, you are not fit enough to be stamped "OK."

Arts and sports: The 2 greatest creations of man aren't even included in the curriculum. In fact, they are considered to be extracurricular activities because the factories didn't need those skills.

Comparison: If your parents have constantly compared you to your friends, neighbours, or cousins, they are simply doing their jobs. The factory expects everybody to be like everybody else, and parents are afraid that only their kid will turn out to be a defective piece. If everybody is becoming an engineer, they want you to become one too.

Questions: In factories, questioning something is a crime. You simply do what you have been asked to do. We are all afraid to ask questions in class, and this fear lasts with us forever, even at work.

Fail: The Indian fear of failure stems from its origin – the school. The word "fail" is synonymous with "failing an exam," which is used to signify a factory defect and is considered a taboo. Far from moulding a mind, the school kills it in cold blood. Let me tell you about an experiment that was conducted in the 1960s by this man called George Land. Land set out to test "Divergent Thinking" in humans. According to Sir Ken Robinson's words, Divergent Thinking is: "The ability to see lots of possible answers to a question. It's not the same thing as creativity, but it is a critical piece of creativity. It's also where new ideas come from. A classic test of one's divergent thinking would be to ask, "what can you do with a paperclip?" Some people – the most gifted of divergent thinkers – can list hundreds of potential functions. Most of us will come up with considerably less than that. The point is to see a range of possibilities in everything, rather than simply look at the fixed title, value, or purpose of something established by others before." George Land conducted a series of experiments on 1,600 school kids between ages 3 and 5, 8 and 10, and 13 and 15 and came up with a soul-stirring discovery. Land found out that initially, 98% of the group ranked as 'divergent thinking geniuses.' By age 10, only 30% of the same group of students qualified to such a level. By age 15, only 10% of the kids were thinking at a "genius" level of divergence. The next time we look at a creative person and label him as an outlier, remember that we were all creative at some point in our life and then that person was just killed in a planned and systematic manner. Cold-blooded.

Most people don't realise the extent of damage that has happened to them in school. How can they? They are barely alive. Like Zombies. They don't realise most of their choices since then are just an illusion. Something or someone else is driving them. Not them.

As the popular quote from one of my favourite movies goes *"The Greatest trick the devil ever pulled was convincing the world that it did not exist"* Our schools are our society's greatest evil.

This finding had left me in a terrible state. The book got published - in a rather dramatic and characteristic chaotic fashion, making my entire publishing team, including a pregnant woman, work non-stop for 48 hours. Just as I had perceived, the book was received really well and quickly became a national bestseller. The two most common feedback I received was that it happened to be the first book many students had read in their lives. Secondly, a lot of them had read the book start-to-end in one go - one of them being this wonderful Sernior World Bank executive who later advised the Prime Minister of India on Higher Education, who read the book in one sitting on his flight to Washington DC. None of it seemed to matter much to me though. I saw all these people walking by and living as if nothing ever happened, but I could see what was happening! What to tell them? I was drinking and smoking away my life. Through the journey of the book and the period after that, for a cumulative period of 3 years, I drank and smoked heavily pretty much every day of my life. I was also sleeping with anyone, really. A woman I met at the Passport office, a girl I met on the train, friends' ex-girlfriends! Debauchery at its wildest. Of course, it took a toll on me. I even made a tweet once which I deleted recently that said, "Suddenly, suicide makes sense." It's not that I was contemplating suicide, but the state in which I was, I could empathise for the first time with what goes through those who commit suicide. Of course, at that point, I had little idea of the role the alcohol, cigarette, and unbridled promiscuity were playing in contributing to my depressive state. It's only much later, after my stint in the monastery, that I would realise how the substances I resorted to escape from my misery were the ones responsible for taking me deeper into it!

Thankfully, I got out of that phase, and of course, it did coincide with the entry of a woman. It always happens. They come, usher in a new phase, and leave. As if their assigned duty was done. This girl happened to read my book and like many others, got in touch with me. Her grandfather was a top bureaucrat at India's Central Bank and worked closely with former Prime Minister Indira Gandhi. Oh man, she definitely did inherit some of those genes. Her parents are top doctors in Mumbai and have some of the top Bollywood celebrities as their clientele. The head of JP Morgan India was her family friend. She literally called her aunty. Take a wild guess where she got her first job? 🤪 😄 When she entered college, she was overweight, had crooked teeth, and major body issues. In an intense body transformation, she chiselled her body into becoming an absolute college babe. She was also pretty problematic though, and I don't really think she made any friends in college. She had a fantastic house and pretty idols she adored.

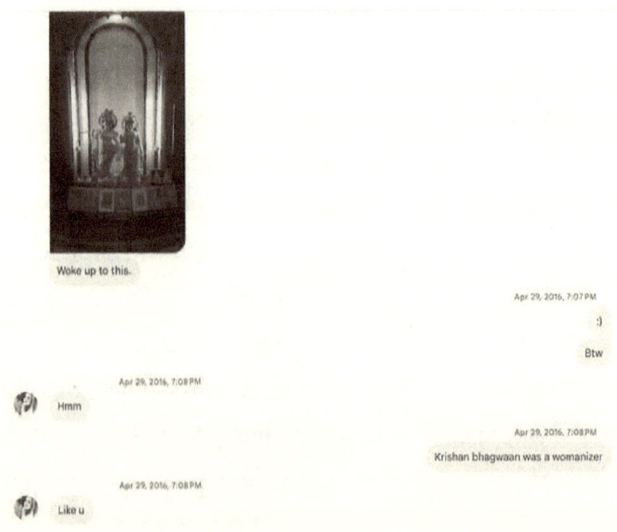

Now, this girl was the founding Chairperson of a local TEDx chapter. TEDx, as you may know, is a globally renowned platform for people of some accomplishment to exchange ideas and inspire others. She insisted I participate as a speaker in the upcoming edition. I wasn't keen because what better do you expect of a man drowned in the enchanting grip of Beauty and Beer? But women usually always have their way with me, so I eventually conceded.

I am preparing and rehearsing every detail of my talk. There couldn't have been a more iconic and symbolic venue - in hindsight I can say now, such a poetic script. More about this in the bonus content. The storyline, the content, My clothes, My shoes, I know exactly what I want to wear and where I'd pick it up from. I don't know why, but I had this sudden urge to wear a watch. Because I never bothered to own one, I had to borrow. I'm reviewing my talk on call, I'm inviting my friends over for rehearsals. I'm having unsettling performance anxiety, so I'm also smoking twice the usual cigarettes. I catch a terrible cold and cough and with just 2 days to go for my talk, she decides to break up. Those days I used to be a very emotionally delicate and sensitive person. I didn't even have my presentation in order. As any responsible guy on the cusp of a breakthrough opportunity should, I placed myself together, worked on my presentation, and continued my rehearsals right? Wrong. I did none of those. Instead, I chose to drink till 4:00 am. After reaching the venue, to make things exponentially worse, I see her walking around. For some reason, she chooses to ignore the fact that I am a guest speaker at the event and misbehaves with me in front of the other guests. I invite a friend over to help me with the presentation and even at the last minute's notice, like an angel, she quickly drops by and just in a few minutes, has my presentation in order. With an awfully broken heart, a presentation that was prepared minutes ago, and totally nervous and dejected, I walk on stage. I don't know what happens to me when I walk on the stage. Something takes over me, words flow and the talk just happens.

As luck may have it, my TEDx talk goes on to become one of the most widely watched talks on education globally. I started receiving comments and emails from kids all over the world. They were more often from the subcontinent - India, Pakistan, Bangladesh, Nepal, and even South-east Asia. I was travelling all over the place to talk, and I could sense how deep a problem this is for everyone.

There was a kid who wrote to me about her intention to commit suicide. That day confirmed what had already started brewing within me - my purpose - to change our education system. . It was so crystal clear. Amongst all the things I had done in life until then, this hit right at the centre of the heart and appealed to the brain too, but there was a problem. I knew I could not solve the problem of education until I had figured out life in some way. Education cannot be divorced from life. As I saw it, it is meant to be an orientation, an introductory session, as is conducted at the time of induction to a new office or university. These kids were new to this world, and they deserved the best induction possible. How am I supposed to provide that when here I am drinking and smoking my life away with a bunch of unanswered questions? I genuinely had no solution, no deep insight about life in order to figure out what the new education system should look like, and then one day, I looked at the mirror, and it was at that moment my life would take a drastic turn.

Please scan this code to unlock $GIC tokens and
Bonus content for this chapter

Question 4 -

Imagine yourself from your early days - before you went to school - unadulterated- how were you and had school not happened and suppressed your inherent intelligence, joy, genius and fearlessness, how would you be today? Imagine and write in great detail. Let's create a new you!

Chapter 05

An 8th Grader God?

If you do the right things for the wrong reasons...
The right things can still happen to you.

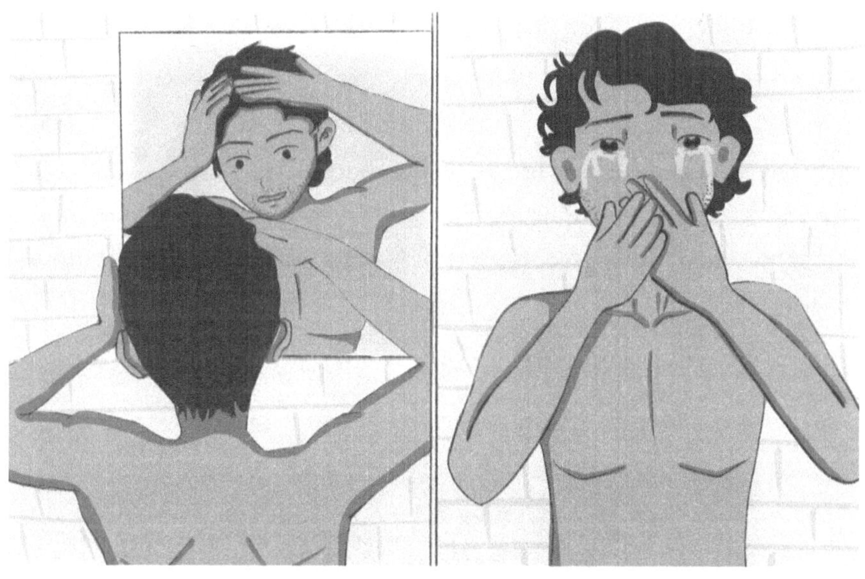

My romance with my hair has been one of the longest and most obsessive affairs of my life. During the making of this book, when Lekha, our illustrator, went through my Instagram and other social media profiles for a reference of how I looked, she scrolled for years back in time and observed that I looked different each time. She didn't know what I looked like! Inevitably, I have a new hairstyle every few weeks. I've been obsessed with Hair Gels, Hair Creams, and Hair Wax from a very young age - a self-diagnosed OCD. And suddenly, here I stood, standing in the mirror, noticing that I, the self-crowned king of hair, was losing hair! 😵 ME? LOSING HAIR? IS THIS WHAT THE MAYANS MEANT BY THE END OF THE WORLD!

It seemed pretty much like that - like the world was ending. I was losing a huge part of me and that I won't be the same anymore. Of course, any responsible guy would respond sensibly, immediately visit a medical expert, alter his diet and lifestyle. Of course, I did none of those. I simply smoked more cigarettes and drank more alcohol. Then I felt I should take medical advice so I went to the doctor. The men's hair loss industry is valued at $4 Billion in the US alone. The doctor prescribed me a bunch of "All-natural" pills that she said would work on my hormones. I wasn't quite comfortable with the idea of taking pills that would mess around with hormones. Na! Nope. Then what? The most intense Planning & Plotting ensued. "Mission Hair Back," one of the most intense secret and high-stake missions in the world was officially ON.

What is a 21st Century Scientist without his share of path-breaking research on well, unverified sources on the internet? Well, they said the internet is a weird place but I had no clue how weird it was. In the course of my research, I encountered a rather strange community of people who had an even stranger prescription for my situation. The community called themselves NoFap (Fap being a colloquial term for Masturbation) and insisted that a bush of thick hair is only one of the many benefits of a simple practice their members swear by: No Masturbation. What does masturbation have to do with hair loss? I had no fucking clue. Neither did I care. During that phase, if you asked me to apply fresh poop from an Antarctic Penguin (< 5 mins old only), I would have done it, okay. The NoFap community was convinced that a man's semen is meant to be preserved within the body and not recklessly shed. They claimed - Retaining the semen has countless benefits including added confidence, a stronger presence, and the only thing I wanted from it then - thicker hair among other benefits. It also claimed that many great men in the past such as Muhammad Ali, Isaac Newton have been practitioners of NoFap. Even Steve Jobs. It seems when Steve Jobs came to India, he learnt about the powers of retaining the semen. In India, ancient wisdom prescribed that the semen is the most potent aspect of a man and the carrier for cosmic energy. So they preserved their semen and with that energy, they did many things. What things? I didn't know. In fact, it is believed that there is nothing a man cannot do who hasn't shed a drop of semen in his life. Steve Jobs was so enchanted with this idea that he also learnt about orgasming without having to ejaculate. When he returned to the US from India, he tried to teach his girlfriend - ways of sexually indulging without having to ejaculate. She freaked out and eventually broke up with him. Curiously, another famous practitioner of Semen Retention was an Indian monk known as Swami Vivekananda. How to introduce him to you now? Swami Vivekananda is probably the most famous Indian of all-time. It's been more than a century since he left but there is no household in India that hasn't heard his name. In India, it is such that if you want to say something wise and want people to listen to you, you simply write anything, add Swami Vivekananda's picture to it and send it as a WhatsApp forward. People will believe you. He was that kind of a figure.

So I felt this thing was worth a shot. It wasn't costing me anything anyway. So I thought, while I'm at it, I'd also refrain from consuming alcohol and cigarettes. As you may have derived by now, I'm a man of great extremes. All or none kind of a guy. I made a 100-day intense plan to regrow my hair: 100 days of no masturbation or anything that would trigger it like pornography, no alcohol, no cigarettes. And I'd apply my intensely researched and formulated TOP SECRET homegrown magical potion for hair growth every day. But as I was just about to start my 100-day challenge, something else happened.

A chance encounter at a bar would lead to me receiving a strange book.

More than half a century ago, there was a rather interesting Meteorology Professor by the name Edward Norton Lorenz. As a boy, Lorenz had a strange fascination for "changes in the weather." Further pursuing his fetish for weather changes, Lorenz received an Undergraduate Degree in Mathematics from Dartmouth in 1938 and a Master's Degree in the same subject from Harvard in 1940. During World War II, he also served the Army Air Corps as a Weather Forecaster and eventually joined MIT as a Meteorology Professor. Oh, also, Lorenz could supposedly talk to Coyotes.

The Computer Program Lorenz was working on factored in 12 variables such as Wind, Speed, Temperature, etc., to produce a certain pattern which predicted the weather. However, this time around, Lorenz made a harmless change: He rounded off one variable from 0.506127 to 0.506. That's it. Hardly a change, right? But this decision of Lorenz turned out to be a turning point in scientific history. Lorenz noticed that the seemingly insignificant rounding-off had drastically transformed the pattern the Computer Program produced. It gave him a simple insight into how the Universe functions: Even an absolutely small change can have unforeseen large consequences, and thus was born the Chaos Theory and the now famous Butterfly effect.

The butterfly effect states that any small change in a complex system, such as the Universe, has a series of unimaginable non-linear impacts on the system. For example, a simple flap of a butterfly wing in Southern India can trigger a series of events that eventually leads to a typhoon in Washington DC.

I told you about Loren and The Butterfly Effect only so you know how, one fine day, a bunch of random 20-something-year-old guys uploaded a video on YouTube that eventually led to a series of events in my life, and now that you are reading this book, maybe your life too.

A bunch of IIT-Kharagpur and IIT-Bombay graduates, trying to find their purpose in life, uploaded a YouTube video in February 2012. The video, a spoof on the popular TV show Roadies, quickly became the first viral video in India, and these guys shot to overnight fame. You know how viral things work. Overnight means, literally, overnight. They went on to produce India's first web series, both of which - Pitcher and TVF Roommate - would go on to become iconic shows of that time. With Netflix & all other OTT players totally absent in India, these guys were the biggest and possibly the only OTT players in India at the time.

At the bar that day was Deepak Kumar Mishra, the star from the first viral video. On enquiring with the waiter, it turned out that this guy had kind of a drinking situation too, and he showed up at the same bar every evening. I got my jholer hat on and approached the guy, showed him the trailer of my book (for which I had generously received a free licence to use an AR Rahman soundtrack from the music studio TIPS).

He loved it and called me over to TVF's office where I first met their boss, Arunabh, who also loved the trailer and the idea of the book. Biswapati Sarkar, another popular face and lead writer (who would then go on to write the Netflix show Kaala Paani), was considered the final authority. Only if he gave a green signal would TVF go ahead with the project. Looks like he loved reading the book too, and just like that, my book was now going to be adapted into a web series by India's biggest digital production house!

The director assigned to the project was, Palash (who later went on to direct the popular show Gullak). Palash is a loving family man with a pet cat, a beautiful and talented wife and a cute son - a sort of picture-perfect family you would see in a newspaper advert! He had lovely parents too. Palash and I had no prior experience with writing a screenplay, so we were in the hunt for a screenplay writer. We interviewed at least 5 different people, and neither Palash nor I were particularly impressed by any of them. Then one day, a friend suggested that I talk to this guy she had recently met during an ad shoot. His name was Abhijeet.

We called Abhijeet over, and we instantly liked him! Just within a few minutes of talking to Abhijeet, we knew we found the guy we were looking for. Unfortunately, though, Abhijeet had to decline the offer reluctantly because of a condition TVF had required him to meet. Abhijeet had a day job, and TVF wanted him to work out of their office only, which meant he would have to quit his job, which seemed impractical for the father of a toddler son, and this project's duration was only about 3-5 months. All 3 of us were very sad as we were desperately hoping things would work out, but it wasn't working out.

That night, I got a call from Abhijeet stating that he would do the project. He told me he won't divulge details (till date he hasn't), but on his way back home, he purchased a copy of my book and read it in one stretch standing on the subway.

He felt it was "a sign." I don't know what he meant, neither did I care. I knew this project was ON. Fuckin' ON. There were three important things I learnt from my stint at TVF . The first one was their business model which thoroughly impressed me - while they were well funded, they never used their VC funds to create any of their shows. That money only went on retaining talent. The shows were produced only when a brand came on board as a sponsor and the work on the show only began once the money touched their bank accounts. Every show they produced were profitable self-sustaining IPs themselves - without having to rely on the VC capital. The second thing I learnt was the art of providing Creative feedback. This was a culture that Arunabh, the founder, had inculcated within the entire team. When it comes to the creative process, it is easy to be vague in giving feedback. Show someone a creative work and it is easy to receive responses such as "Oh, maybe you can add some wow element to it" "Oh, can you make it more fun?" "Can you make it more viral?" These feedback usually serves no purpose at all. The feedback sessions in TVF left me so impressed - they were very specific and actionable where the creator would know exactly what to work on and change. The third takeaway? We shall arrive at that soon.

Days went by, and I continued going to TVF's office, working on the OTT adaptation of my debut book, retaining my semen. With a magic potion on my head that was now beginning to spread its menace in their office. One day, both Abhijeet and the director Palas raised an alarm for an unmissable foul smell in the cabin. I knew exactly what they were talking about but pretended not to 😌 😇

Abhijeet and I became close. I think we both loved talking and listening. Over the years, I've heard all kinds of people speak. Once, someone confessed to me about having murdered someone and since then absconding from their hometown. Somebody I met on the train was having an affair with a married man. Somebody I shared an Uber with confessed about deriving sadist pleasure from watching other people get tortured. This way, I have been privy to many secrets. First, I shared with Abhijeet my NoFap experiment, and that got him to open up about his life in a big way. He told me about this phase in his life where he left his prestigious college (IIT-BHU) in search of something he had no full idea about. The search took him to many places, including a guru's ashram where he had seen even dogs meditating! Later, disgruntled with the guru, he left his ashram and after a long and painful search, he claimed to have found his answers in another Guru who went by the name Meher Baba. This entire business of gurus and meditation, et al. was getting a bit too much for me to digest. "Where is Meher Baba?" I asked him. "He left his body in 1969," was his response that I felt was pretty strange. "Why can't you just say he died? What do you mean by leaving his body?" I thought in my head. "How come he found his Guru in someone who isn't even around?" I wondered. Then I assumed, maybe, this guy must be smitten by Meher Baba's philosophies and teachings so I inquired about them. "Well, he remained silent for most of his life," was his bizarre response. Now, an integral aspect of being a good listener is the ability to listen to a person without judging them, but this seemed a little too much for me to not judge. A young, educated man, falling for a Guru and that too when the Guru is not even around and neither had much to say or teach while he was around. I mean, how? And more importantly, why? I remember gossiping with my friend Tanush later that day. It baffled me as to how educated young Indians like Abhijeet ended up falling for such ridiculousness.

Like this, the days passed by effortlessly. There was never even an iota of conflict in my head about breaking my oath of 100-day celibacy mid-way. Just like that, at the snap of the finger, I moved myself from ultimate debauchery to abstinence literally overnight. I guess a man will go to any extent to save everything and everyone he loves, of course, including his hair! Till date, I can't say for sure whether it was placebo, or the NoFap, or my magic potion or a mix of them all, but there was an unbelievably tremendous growth of hair on my scalp. It was like a miracle unfolding in front of me (well, top of me tbh) and everyone else at home could see it as well. Not just re-growth, but it had the kind of volume and thickness I hadn't felt in a long time. It was like the hair I remember from my earlier days. I think my mom was perhaps more shocked and relieved than I was, which is strange because this should have been a matter of great relief and accomplishment for me, but there was something else that was brewing within me and I didn't know what to make of it. Almost like an unforeseen and unanticipated side-effect that my Planning & Plotting I had never accounted for, not even by the wildest estimates. In fact, it almost seemed like the hair growth was the side-effect. The real deal was something else. I ignored it as a possible hallucination.

Days progressed, and one day, an event I had no control over brought the web series to a halt. The company found itself in the midst of a controversy and this had put a break on many projects within the company, including mine. At the time of leaving, Abhijeet said he was wanting to offer me a gift in case I was okay to receive it. "Of course,"

I said. He wanted to gift me a copy of Meher Baba's book called God Speaks, which contained his life's important teachings. I enjoyed reading books anyway, so I was happy to receive it, and I did. I didn't somehow get myself to read it immediately, but it was a nice farewell gift.

Something miraculous happened at the time which taught me a very important third lesson which would take me some more time to truly imbibe but also happens to be one of crypto's core principles-DON'T TRUST ANYONE. This is what happened - The TVF office had 2 floors - the ground floor where the creative team resided, and the business team sat on the first floor. I worked on the ground floor with the creative team, and this included some of the top actors, writers, and directors in the Indian OTT space of the day, but never did anyone make me feel like an outsider, including Arunabh, the founder who visited the floor occasionally. They were some of the most unassuming, humble, loving, and brilliant people within the OTT space on that floor. Since I was mainly hanging out with these folks, I assumed the guys on the top floor would be the same, but always beware of the business folks! I was given a contract to sign, which I blindly did given the relation I had developed with the guys and the consequent trust that arose from it. You can call it a stupid move, but there was also a strange intelligence to it. The Indian legal system is a mess and heavily understaffed for a nation of over a billion people. Fighting any legal case drains resources and a huge amount of time, so I felt the deal relied more on trust than the law. At that time, there was no scenario in my head where I imagined I could be cheated. After the project was put on the back burner, the business guys went back on the agreed terms of engagement, and I did not receive the 2 remaining instalments I was supposed to as compensation for granting them the rights to my book. Only then I decided to read the contract, and man, I was massively duped! Almost conned, legally. The contract stated that I had irrevocably granted them the rights to my book for perpetuity and that it could be used in any way and medium they deemed fit, and I had no claim on any further remuneration whatsoever. In exchange, they would pay me a paltry sum, which also they held back on. This had broken me then in a big way. I had never imagined that I would face a betrayal of this kind. I urged the creative guys I was working with, including my director, to do something about it, and he tried his best. Then one day, yet another miracle happened. It is times like these, you cannot help yourself from thinking about an unknown force. It may or may not be God, but how do you explain such events in your life?

One day, I received a call from the legal team at TVF, and it seems that they had misplaced the contract and that they would require me to sign a new one! Can you believe it? CAN YOU BELIEVE IT? What are the odds of that happening?! Life offered me another shot to undo the damage I did the first time! Of course, I got legal counsel this time and made sure the contract was signed, keeping in mind my personal interest and that of the book. I also received my balance payment immediately. But while all of this happened on the outside, something miraculous (or ridiculous?) continued to brew within me. It was getting stronger by the day, and it was so bizarre that I couldn't even share it with anyone. So instead of ignoring it, I decided to explore it this time around. Of course, I went to the least judgemental (or is it?) source for an answer.

I started having this creepy feeling that the world as we know may not be real. I know it sounds crazy, but it is what it is! What am I to do? I did ignore it at first, but then the feeling just got stronger and stronger. When I was involved in any activity, everything was fine, but the moment I just sat by myself, I would just be absorbed by this overwhelming sense that this world is not real. What do I really mean by that? Lol, I wish I knew! I wish somebody, anybody could tell me what was happening to me! I didn't know anything beyond the feeling that something seemed off and that all of this could be a dream! Maybe a Computer Simulation? A video game! For all you know, our God could be an 8th grader school kid, and we could all be part of their school Metaverse project, and as soon as they finish showcasing their project, all of this would end. Could you say for sure that this couldn't be true? Of course, not! Where could the Control Panel for this creation be so as to hack it? Is it hidden inside a secret cave? In the Amazon Forests? In the Himalayas?

Interestingly, one of the first Google results that caught my attention had to do with Elon Musk. Elon Musk is supposedly a firm believer of the fact that we couldn't be part of base reality and that we could all be a part of a Matrix, maybe a computer simulated code.

"If you assume any rate of improvement at all, games will eventually be indistinguishable from reality," Musk said before concluding, "We're most likely in a simulation."

It seems serious academic discussions around this really began with a 2003 paper by Nick Bostrom. In it, the University of Oxford philosopher stated: If there are long-lived technological civilisations in the universe, and if they run computer simulations, there must be a huge number of simulated realities complete with artificial-intelligence inhabitants who may have no idea they're living inside a game — inhabitants like us, perhaps.

I think Elon also had a start-up (maybe still does). I think it's called Neura link (or something else), and one of the main objectives of the start-up is to "get us out of the Matrix." I don't know why, but the aesthetics of it all didn't appeal to me at all. I thought Elon was cute. Like a child. Enthusiastic at best, but he didn't really know a thing about this. I have always placed a very high value on the importance of aesthetics in my life. When I say aesthetics, I don't just mean the look of something but more about the feel of it. Of Objects, of music, of words, of clothes, of approach, of mindset. For me, everything animate and inanimate has a certain aesthetic. When I heard Elon speak on the subject and looked at his ways (it involved wires, and planting chips on the brain etc.), it all seemed so ugly to me. Like an aesthetic nightmare. I felt whoever the creator of this world is, they too have a tremendous sense of aesthetics. The highest of them all. I mean, look at the glorious sunrise and the infinite possibilities it brings, the lustfully irresistible body of a woman, the intimate silence of the night, or the hypnotic beauty of a Peacock's feather! Absolute Aesthetic Masterpieces. And if there could indeed be a way out of his/her own creation, it too had to have the creator's approval, and somehow, I didn't feel that the creator programmed the exit in such an ugly and exclusive way. That people should be able to afford it and they have to go to this one guy and insert some wires in their head or chips in their brain and it involves computers and all that jazz. Then what about people before computers were invented? What about people who cannot afford it? Don't they have the right out of this Matrix? Is the creator so capitalist and elitist? It just didn't "feel right." Know what I mean? So anyway, I felt this guy is cute like a child, and I just moved on. Then one day, during my routine gossip calls, Tanush had an OTT show recommendation for me out of the blue. I always go to Tanush for recommendations on what to watch. He just has a 100% track record of suggesting some really cool stuff. This time he suggested that I watch a newly released series called Westworld. It was written by Jonathan Nolan, Christopher Nolan's brother and his frequent collaborator. Pretty much seemed like a no-brainer decision to me! I started watching it immediately. It had really interesting characters and people whose lives you get quickly involved with, and then suddenly it is revealed that these people and their world are actually not real but a creation of a company that created it for the sake of entertainment of its guests. It was like a theme park. And then suddenly some of these robots, characters, people, become sentient. They become conscious, and that's when the show takes a dramatic twist.

When I watched this, I felt like I was being played. This theme of the world not being real is literally following me everywhere! Even the series that I am watching! You know the part I enjoy the most with women? It's not the sex or the orgasm. I mean, it's a great driving force to work towards, but the tease? Uff, I love it. I love to tease a woman till she can't take it anymore, and then I tease her more. The sweet pain of the tease should become so intolerable that she just wants to be destroyed by it.

And in some way, in this phase, life was doing that with me. Almost like a retribution for what I do! And guess what, I loved every bit of it.

What is this that was happening to me? Is the world indeed unreal? Is this all a dream? It teased me but didn't give me an answer, and it was for me to find out. And I hope, it's a pain that everyone goes through. There is one moment that for me represents the entire episode - I was just headed for a shower, and as I crossed the mirror, I couldn't resist looking myself at the mirror. It was strange - I felt alive - in fact, I realised I was alive - how do I know I am alive? Who is the guy looking at the mirror? Who created this guy? Who created the guy who made this guy? It all lasted just for a few seconds, and at the end of it, I burst out in laughter - of amazement - of wonderment - will it ever be possible to know? Of course, at that moment I didn't know that sometime later, life would be kind enough to offer clarity - not without a fair share of pain and struggle of course.

Over the next few months, I lived as if nothing else existed in my life. Just a deep desire to find an answer to this problem. I read countless books, watched countless documentaries, heard countless people, but the answer never came. More tease. Then the pressure was also mounting on me to find a job. How am I supposed to find a job or do anything when this is happening to me? I mean when the basis of my life itself is in question, how am I supposed to do anything else? Just then, my father got diagnosed with cancer. Well, it came as a shock but not a surprise. He had a notorious reputation of neglecting his health which was quite the opposite of my mother, one of the healthiest members of the family. She had never been to a hospital. Given that the entire family was occupied with this emergency, the pressure on me to find a job had been paused, which allowed me more time to explore the mystery. More desperate attempts to comprehend but to no real result. More reading, more listening, more watching. This time also some bizarre body experiments. I went on a bizarre diet I read online and lost 6 kgs within a week or 9 days. Although they were used to my antics, it freaked people around me so I stopped. Still no answer. My first major breakthrough happened with a book. Actually books. In fact, not even the books but its author. I read this book called **Sapiens** by Yuval Noah Harari which now I guess is a modern-day classic. The book, as its tagline perfectly summarises, is a "brief history of mankind." Now, as a matter of principle, I never read history books nor do I indulge myself much in that subject because it is a futile exercise. I have seen how skewed and biased our understanding of the present is so I never trusted humans to make accurate sense of the past. Because our interpretation of history is always based on what we know and what we know makes only a minuscule part of the actual picture. Now, let's say a totally new civilisation arises 1000 years from now and somehow somebody unearthed a copy of a Harry Potter book. Now this guy will assume the book to be true and make a God of Harry Potter - a totally fictitious character. What they don't know is that humans in the past invested themselves heavily in entertainment and made up stuff just for the purpose of merriment! But that guy uses it as proof of an ancient human civilisation. And the worst part is both, what we know and what we don't know make only a small part of our understanding of the universe. What makes an infinite part is what we don't even know what we don't know! Confused? See, For instance, let's take sports as an example, you may say that you know about cricket but you don't know anything about football. So you are clear about what you know and you don't know. But you don't even know that there is a sport called Chess Boxing that you don't even know you didn't know about it!

But anyway, in spite of this understanding, I still chose to read Sapiens because Tanush recommended it to me. Plus, this book was more about a generic history of how humans became the most dominant animals on the planet than a specific commentary. It was a book that fascinated me like no other. Like every book I read, it was not just about reading but sort of an affair. The author spoke about the importance of agriculture, and particularly how growing wheat contributed to this evolution. It spoke about the role gossip and storytelling played in humans becoming such a dominant force. More than the content itself, I was extremely fascinated by how the author looked at the world. I loved the lens with which he was able to see things, and I felt it was phenomenal. So naturally, when the sequel to the book came, I wasted no time in grabbing it. I enjoyed the second book more than the first, but it wasn't the book itself that was a turning point in my life as much as the opening page of the book turned out to be.

In the book, he had acknowledged and thanked "his teacher" SN Goenka. Now SN Goenka is clearly an Indian name, and I knew this author is an Israeli guy, a homosexual, grows his own food, and lives with his partner. Who is this Indian teacher now, and why is he thanking him? Turns out SN Goenka is a teacher of a very popular Buddhist technique called Vipassana, and as part of the training, one is supposed to spend 10 days in silence without any form of communication or access to a mobile phone or any other device and meditate for 10 hours a day. Turns out Yuval is a seasoned practitioner of Vipassana and, in fact, does it for 60 straight days in a year. When the new calendar year arrives, he plans his 60-day trip to India for his Vipassana, and the rest of his calendar year revolves around that. Now, until that point, even the thought of meditating never occurred to me. I never felt the need, neither did I know why one meditates, nor did I know anyone personally who used to meditate, nor did I find any meditator impressive enough to follow them. Even the ones in popular culture, like Buddha, I admired, and they also appealed to me aesthetically, but the kind of celibate and dry life he lived never encouraged me enough to pursue it. In fact, this may seem odd, but my favourite drunk thing to watch during my stay in Bangalore was this particular documentary the BBC made on Buddha. It was very enchanting to watch, and I watched it multiple times, particularly when I was drunk. There is also a piece of music that was used in the documentary that I hunted down. It's called Open or The Buddha by Michael Bacon. That became a staple listen too. But it all seemed like a good thing to admire from a distance. But for the first time, with Yuval, I found someone who appealed to me enough to explore meditation. So I quickly looked up Vipassana. Turns out that there is an elaborate application, selection process, and a waiting period and is conducted in a select cluster of monasteries located all over the world. As luck may have it, the main monastery, the HQ and the most sought after centre in the world is located just a 3-hour drive from my home city, Mumbai! So I applied with great enthusiasm and curiosity for a programme that was to be conducted 3 months later, patiently waiting for my acceptance. While that happened, I began to read more about this strange world of spirituality. The first book I picked up was the one Abhijeet gifted me, but I didn't follow a word in it! It seemed all too abstract for me, so after trying to read a few pages, I put it back. I read a few other things on the internet, and as you know, the internet is home to all things strange, so some of the stories I read involving some famous saints and sages of India seemed too fantastical to be true, so I enjoyed reading them albeit with some scepticism. I could do this carefree without any pressure of a job hanging over me because my father's treatment was still on, so I was expected to engage with that for now. My NoFap and abstinence from other things would go on for a few more days - at least till the Vipassana programme. Then one day I received an email confirming my participation for the upcoming Vipassana programme! I was elated! I didn't even know what I was elated about! It seemed like getting admission into your dream university, but at least you know what a dream university will get you in life. I didn't even know what I was going to receive in these 10 days. I informed my mother about the programme, and it didn't take much convincing really. I think it had more to do with the family being drained off my father's treatment, and she saw it as a well-deserved break.

The only preparation I did in the run-up to my Vipassana was to listen to the music from The Buddha documentary I mentioned earlier. I used to always say this half-jokingly jokingly that music is perhaps man's greatest creation after beer. I have a very intimate relationship with music, and I listen to all kinds of music. I never paid much attention to the lyrics; in fact, I always make up the lyrics.

I don't just listen to music but feel them, so genres never really mattered to me. Right from the massy mirth of Bollywood music to the serenity of western classical to the profundity of Indian classical. I can just experience different aspects of life - different worlds - just by listening to the right music. In preparation for my Vipassana programme, that piece of music became an intimate partner. I could have well made it my theme song. The mystery, the longing, the tease, the playful wisdom. That song offered me everything, and just like that, I entered the monastery, and it was a glorious sight! Surrounded by mountains and welcomed by slightly solemn-looking but extremely dedicated volunteers. I observed there were participants from outside India as well. I remember particularly interacting with a participant from Bangladesh who found one particular habit of Indians fascinating. Drinking water from tumblers in public water tanks without touching the lips. He said he hadn't seen it anywhere else! It's funny how even the most seemingly insignificant habits have so many geo-cultural variations!

The programme started by segregating participants into different groups who would go through the programme in different rooms. I think segregation was done based on parameters such as socio-economic backgrounds. Later, I realised this was not elitism but an unfortunate necessity. Because the programme was generously offered free of cost in the beautiful set up of the mountains, along with free meals, of course, there were a lot of participants from local communities who tended to belong to certain socio-economic groups. They came there not to participate but just to have fun, often breaking programme rules and disrupting the experience for others. At the start, we were clearly told that once the programme begins, the gates would be locked, and participants would have to complete all 10 days and would not be allowed to leave under any circumstances. Everyone was offered a chance to leave the programme before the start itself. One guy chose to accept the offer and left.

There were tiny huts that could accommodate 2 people each and had one bathroom. We were randomly assigned rooms, and my roommate turned out to be a man in his 50s. Warm and welcoming face with a sincere smile. He ran a hotel business in the extremely popular temple town of a very famous saint in India - Shirdi's Sai Baba. To my disappointment, the room had an Indian toilet - something that I had been averse to all my life and despite having travelled through remote parts of India for my first book, I somehow always avoided using the Indian toilet, preferring the comfort of its western counterpart. I requested a change of room, but it was politely declined. Accepting my temporary urinal fate for 10 days, I went to sleep with great anticipation. My programme was to start the following morning, but I began to experience horror the night before.

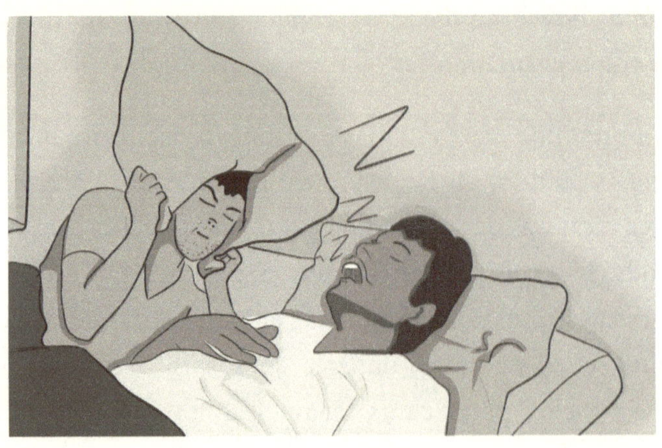

Turns out my roommate was a champion snorer. I kid you not, I am willing to bet a sizable amount on the fact that he could be the loudest snorer in the world. If there ever was a championship for snoring, he wouldn't be announced the winner but the judge! There could, in fact, be championships named after him. It was reminiscent of the journey for my first book. If any of you have read it, you would know I faced the same problem during my train journey for the travels of the first book, and the book, of course, turned out to be a huge milestone in my life. Good omen maybe? It was obviously not what I was thinking at the time. I woke the guy up and gestured about my discomfort. He acknowledged, and then it stopped. Thank goodness! But after a few mins, he would start again. After interrupting his sleep a few times, he got slightly angry and broke his silence by telling me that he had a disorder and that he took some tablets for his snoring problem. In fact, after my multiple complaints, he took one right in front of me but to no relief :/ Useless medicine only.

So after a night of no sleep, a disturbing morning routine in an Indian toilet, I arrived for my first session of the programme. It would be unfair of me to reveal anything about the beautiful practice, and hence I shall refrain. I just couldn't get myself to meditate. I mean, meditating was still a higher-order problem. I was barely able to sit comfortably without the convenience of a chair. Plus, I was sleep-deprived. So, my first day just went like that - disturbed.

Once again, I was trying to find sleep at night. Plus, I haven't slept for an entire day, so I assumed that I would find deep sleep, totally oblivious to this bulldozer pretending to be a human. Alas, but this construction site ASMR had no pause button! Remember when you are watching a reel or a TikTok and you have to drop your phone for some urgent activity, and that damn reel or TikTok just keeps playing on loop, and you can't do anything about it? These are times you wonder how dumb smartphones can be. So I took my pillow, blanket, and decided to move out of my hut and sleep outside, but guess what! This was not an ASMR, na na, it was a god-damn concert! I could hear it even outside the hut. So I went further out, to an alternate universe, just to be safe, and luckily, I couldn't hear it anymore. Heaving a sigh of relief, I slept. But then a different sound disrupted my sleep this time, that of mosquitoes! These damn buzzing safety pins, barely the size of a happy dent and audacity of a honey badger!

I came to terms with the fact that I would go another night without sleep. The following morning, I did write a small note to the volunteers about my situation - we were allowed to do this only in exceptional circumstances, and clearly I was having one. I was told all rooms are fully booked, and as soon as there was any availability, they would let me know. After 4 sleepless nights, I finally got a new room. The original inhabitant literally had a prison break. The organisers were being honest when they said the gates will be locked. It literally was. This guy was so desperate and resolved to leave that the volunteers had to push him over the gate just so he doesn't become a nuisance for everyone else. I moved into my new room, and it was gorgeous! It was one of the newly constructed rooms, I had no roommate, had a clean western toilet, and a gorgeous view of the mountain straight outside my hut! I finally had one of the most well-deserved sleeps of my life.

In some way, my Vipassana programme was only starting now, but no matter how hard I tried, I just couldn't meditate. My mind and thoughts were all over the place. My body made things even more difficult, but the thing I looked forward to the most were the evening sessions where they would play a video of SN Goenka talking, and I found them intellectually very stimulating. I learnt a great deal from those sessions. One day while meditating (or rather, while trying), a random bizarre thought stuck deep within somewhere inside me came up to the surface, and I just struggled to ignore it. Any spiritual process is like a deep surgery. It means that wounds need to be open, cleansed, and then once the work is done, it needs to be closed for healing. That's why in any spiritual process, including Vipassana, it's said, no matter what, don't leave it mid-way because old wounds will be opened, and it may not be easy. If one leaves mid-way before the surgery is complete, then you essentially move around with an open wound, which makes things more dangerous for you and others around you. This is exactly what happened to me during Vipassana. An old wound resurfaced, and I couldn't handle it, no matter how hard I tried. It kept haunting me, so I sort of left the surgery mid-way. No, I did not escape or even try to, but I broke my noble silence in the last 2 days and joined the gang of mischief-mongers who were notorious for not taking the programme seriously. The wound was still open, but I could at least distract myself by talking and not taking notice of it.

I had a series of curious experiences towards the end of my stay, oddly for which I am tempted to take the course again at a later time. Post my mental breakdown and with the Assistant teacher's consent, I stopped meditating. Like a typical backbencher, I would simply sit at the back of the hall and watch everyone else meditate in front of me (because there is nothing else to do. You either meditate or watch others meditate). On the 9th day, I observed my body vibrate back and forth like a pendulum. For 2 straight hours, I just sat and observed vibrations penetrate my body (Stop calling me a freak, will you). This ended as soon as everyone in the hall stopped meditating. It happened throughout the 9th and 10th day.

Vipassana as a technique is extremely beautiful, but it was my inability as a beginner to experience it to the fullest. Although I couldn't get much hang of the practice, I learnt a lot of new things about the world of spirituality and Vipassana in those days. I immediately blogged about it, which a seasoned Vipassana meditator read and was impressed by. I felt good that at least those 10 days of suffering amounted to something indeed :) Sharing excerpts from that blog here:

The beautiful Pagoda at Dhamma Giri, set against the hills, Igatpuri.

What is spirituality, and how is it different from religion?

Religion is about creating social order and deals with humans on a collective level, whereas spirituality deals with humans on an individual level with its focus on you.

Religion has played a significant role in evolving humans into the most dominant (and dangerous) animal on the planet. In the form of stories, religion has long told us what is 'good' and 'bad' and that if we do the right things, we go to heaven; or hell otherwise. For instance, humans prefer to be loyal to their partners not out of fear of the law but out of fear of doing something that is 'wrong,' 'bad,' and immoral. Without monogamy, human society will have to confront unprecedented chaos.

Albeit important, all of these are eventually subjective truths: What may be 'immoral' for one may appear perfectly reasonable to another.

Spirituality, on the other hand, deals with the objective truth about you, your body, and your mind, but there is a catch: Spirituality cannot be understood but only experienced. In fact, it dismisses intellectual indulgence (condescendingly calls it "intellectual entertainment" or "intellectual drama") and puts foremost emphasis on experiential learning.

Orgasm: "Intellectual entertainment" vs "Experiential learning"

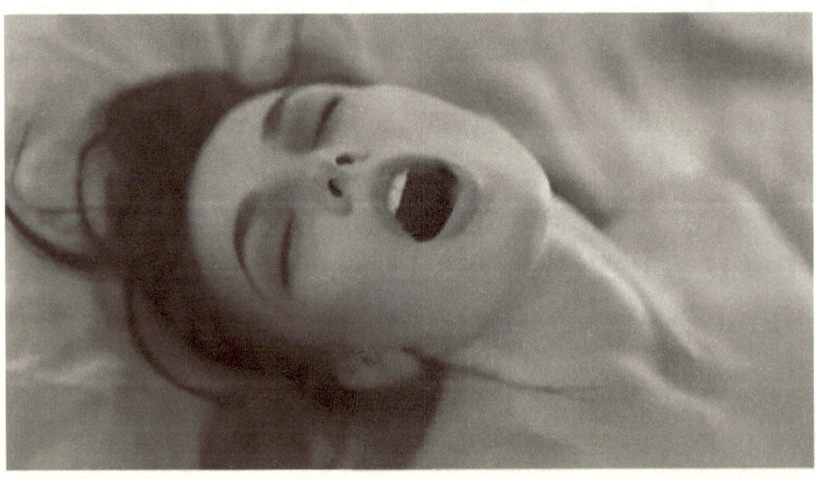

If you are reading this, I am going to assume you have experienced at least one orgasm in life: by virtue of self-pleasure or otherwise. Imagine you were to explain what an orgasm feels like to a friend who hasn't experienced it yet. You will feed her with all possible intellectual data/ analogies to best describe an orgasm and what it feels like. Far from experiencing an orgasm, the friend, being a gifted intellectual, goes on to conduct significant research on the biochemical reactions that occur when one orgasms and the effect it has on different regions of the brain. Happy with the progress she made on the topic, she also publishes countless research papers and Facebook updates on her findings. She goes to bed every night pretending to know so much about an orgasm. All of this is but only her 'intellectual drama.' If she truly wants to understand what an orgasm feels like, she must simply experience it!

Similarly, spirituality claims that the best way to understand life, your body, and mind, is not by cutting it open and indulging in "intellectual drama," but by experiencing it. It makes claims about the human body and mind that, at best, appear fascinatingly mysterious and, at worst, bizarre. For instance, it claims that what you consider yourself is changing to the extent of 2 trillion times per second. So what really are you? It claims that it is possible to transcend your physical and mental barriers to experience another dimension. Given that you and I are nowhere close to experiencing any of these mystic claims, it only serves the purpose of "intellectual entertainment" for us. So how does one experience all these mysterious possibilities? There exists a technology in place, and it's called meditation.

Whether you own an iPhone or an Android, the science behind it is essentially the same. All of them harness different technologies, and you eventually use the technology that suits you best. Similarly, there exist multiple meditation technologies, all of which operate on the same science. Vipassana is one such lost technology invented by The Buddha (at its peak, used by seekers across the subcontinent and beyond, till as far as Afghanistan and China) and today rekindled across the globe by S.N. Goenka. It is possibly the purest and a fairly extreme form of meditation.

What does Vipassana mean?

Vipassana means "to see things as they are." Let me simplify that for you.

The photo you see below is the original copy of the Constitution of India.

If you are Indian, possible reactions may include: "OMG! This is such a great document,"

"This is the holy grail that all Indians live by." If you look at the object "as it is," you will notice nothing "great" or "holy" about the object per se. The chemical composition of the paper is the same as that of any other: it contains Cellulose, Hemi-cellulose, and Lingin. Any search for "great" or "holy" chemical in it is a wasteful exercise. What remains is just "A book with text written on it." Similarly, if someone abuses you, Vipassana will train your mind to process the abuse as merely a stream of words. It claims that it is only your reaction to the mere stream of words that gives it undue importance. Whether or not you grasp these examples on an intellectual level is futile, but with its technology, Vipassana and other meditation techniques urge you to experience it.

Closing words: If you have ever been a gamer, you'd be familiar with the idea of cheat codes, a bunch of hacks known initially to a select few that help them through the game while others struggle. For me, the world of spirituality and meditation is just that: hacks currently known to a select few. As far as Vipassana is concerned, I believe it requires a certain amount of intellectual and emotional maturity. I will recommend it to anyone at least 25 years of age and/or with prior exposure to other simpler forms of meditation. While you try other technologies, I will urge you to experience Vipassana at least once in this lifetime.

Now that I look at my life - almost like a spectator while writing this book and having indulged deeply into the world of spirituality, I find it appalling that the version of me from those days, with absolutely no known prior experience with any form of spiritual practice, could write all this. It is baffling. There was one teaching of Buddha which I couldn't come to terms with, though and this principle would become a cornerstone of my later spiritual conflict - Buddha says that Life is suffering and Nirvana - the ultimate freedom from the cycles of birth and death- is an end to this suffering - and hence humans should make it their highest goal. My experience of life was in full contrast with what the Buddha said - far from seeing it as any form of suffering, I always saw it as a beautiful gift. Why would one want to seek an escape from this gift?

After my Vipassana experience, I had mentally entered this curious world of spirituality. I was convinced that the solution to my education system problem and understanding of life in general definitely lay there. For some reason, I kept going back to that book Abhijit gifted me, but I didn't follow a thing. I called him one day to express my confusion. He laughed and said, "When Baba was in his body, a lot of people would make the same complaints, and he would smile at them and gesture to them to keep it under their pillow at the time of sleeping."

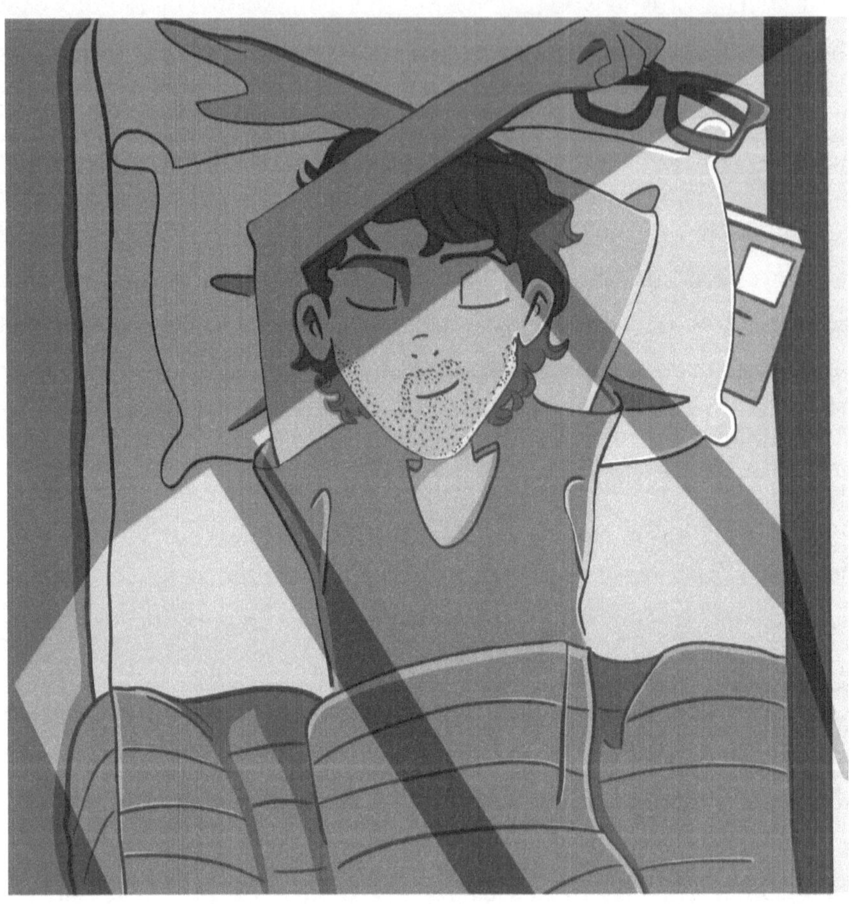

Even though I had opened up, this suggestion seemed too ridiculous to me, so I ignored it. But the pain of not knowing? Uff, it was consuming me every moment. One day, I received an invite to talk at a college in the small town of Sangli in my home state of Maharashtra. Because they had no airport, the organisers had booked me a sleeper bus. My desperation for answers had become too acute, and I was willing to do anything. I thought I would carry this book with me during the trip. I hadn't made up my mind on keeping it under the pillow yet. The bus arrived, the time had come to sleep, and I did the unimaginable. I kept the book under my pillow. When I woke up the next morning…

Please scan this code to unlock $GIC tokens and
Bonus content for this chapter

Question 5 -

What is the single biggest attachment you have - Of which, even the thought of taking it away from you gives you the chills? How do you see yourself if it is taken away from you and how do you see others responding to you if it is taken away from you?

Chapter 06

When The Saints Go Marching In

Man proposes; God Disposes
And Thats How, My Beloved Friend,
Reality Makes Way For The Truth

When I woke up that day, with the book under my pillow, everything seemed normal. "Seemed" - that's the key. Nothing had evidently changed for me, which was rather deceiving because at least one thing clearly had. It felt like a woman's haircut. Days of planning and hours of execution in the salon and a lot is supposed to have changed, but to the male eye, very little is evident. In the same way, months of seeking, tortuous body experiments, countless books, sacrifices, documentaries, and a 10-day painful meditation retreat later, boom, my "world being unreal" conundrum had just vanished. Poof! Just like that. Literally overnight. And I didn't seem to care or even notice.

The students and the organising committee that had invited me for the talk were kind in their hospitality, as they always are. If time permits, I love to hop on a bike with one of the students and go around the city, particularly to try some local street food! That's not it. My first book had opened a world of possibilities for me, but one thing I cherish the most is that it was responsible for one of my life's most intimate and significant affairs - travelling. Looking back, I cannot emphasise enough how transformational travelling solo has been for me. I started travelling solo first only while working on The Great Indian Obsession and since then it has become an inseparable part of my life. When any young boy or girl comes to me for advice, particularly "spiritual," I always ask them to travel alone. We will elaborate more in detail later as to why. But one aspect is when you travel alone, you mimic who you really are - a solo traveller in this rather adventurous and painfully mysterious journey of life. But travelling needs resources, right? A question people ask me often is how did I manage to do that in my early 20s? There are 2 reasons really - One is my ever-available "jholer" hat which enables me to somehow find a way and then the second reason got to be this now recurring strange force for which I had no name - it had been kind in arranging all the travels for me. How? When an invitation for a talk comes my way, I first open Google Maps of the campus and look what's around and then travel to all those places after my talk is done. What about the money? Well, whichever college I got invited to usually didn't have the budget to pay (just student body things. It helped that I was practically a part of every student body in my college to understand these nuances) so I would instead ask them to arrange for my flight tickets to and fro as well as my stay (usually a guest house in their own campus) which usually turned out to be a reasonable deal for them. I then carried a few copies of my book which I would sign and sell to the audience after my talk. With flight tickets and spare cash in hand from my book sales, a chunk of my travel expenses usually got covered and thus by extending my stay by a few days after every talk, I have been fortunate enough to travel to diverse geographies!

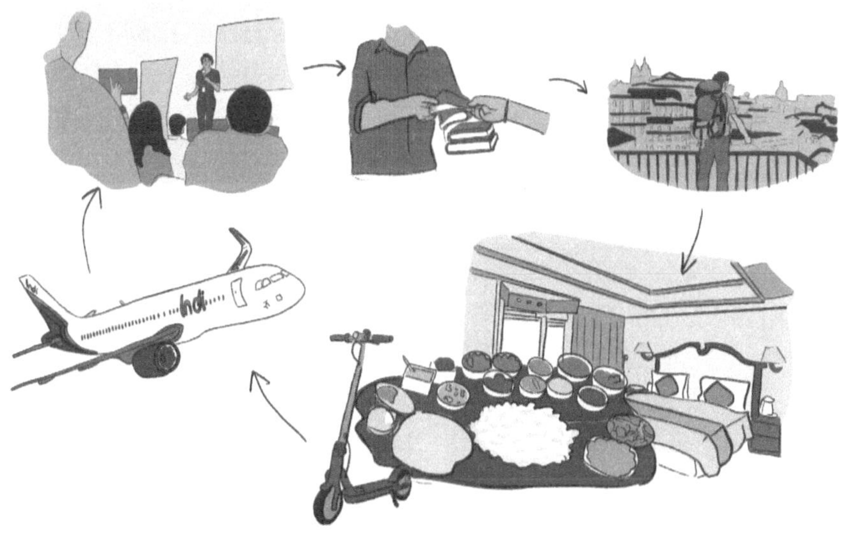

Travel alters you in more ways than one. It started changing how I looked, how I spoke, how I dressed, what I valued.

This particular talk, as it was relatively closer to home, I did not intend to travel much after the talk and instead planned to return back the same day. But the guy who left for the talk wouldn't exactly be the guy who returned from the talk. The talk went quite well actually - the talk was scheduled for the evening, the intimacy of which I really enjoy, the audience had a lot of questions to ask. There is a photo from this talk of me signing books as one of my Facebook cover photos. There was a huge queue for a signed copy. However, something strange happened after the talk though. One of the kids comes to me and tells me that he found one part particularly intriguing in my talk - the one in which I talked about death. Well, that's great but here is the thing - I HAD ABSOLUTELY NO RECOLLECTION of talking about DEATH, that too in a freaking ENGINEERING COLLEGE. What on the Milky Way was that? It had never been a regular (or even irregular) feature of any of my previous talks so I have no clue what this guy is talking about?

What Death, man? What the hecking heck? I kept thinking about this throughout my walk from the auditorium to the room. Totally oblivious to what the kids accompanying me were saying, my mind was constantly occupied by that death incident.

I felt it was too risky and potentially embarrassing to ask these kids what else I spoke about. What if I mentioned that the Dinosaurs' extinction is just a hoax created by believers of the Earth is round theory?! I reached my room and first saw my mother's text enquiring about how my talk was received, but instead of responding to her question, I felt the need to finally ask her something. Maybe even confront her obstinately? I wanted to know what happened in my childhood that day when I was taken to the hospital and why a tablet was fed to me for years after that. After much hesitation, she relented, and what I heard was revealing for sure, but it barely surprised me. Before I tell you what she told me and how my life metamorphosed into something that I had never imagined, it is important to establish how I was before that fateful morning.

After the success of my start-up, book, TEDx talk, and the following travels, a certain and almost characteristic arrogance had seeped in. I tasted back-to-back success in everything I put my hand on. It contributed immensely to my sense of power that everything went largely as per my "Planning & Plotting." I loved every damn bit of it! Uff, the gratifying joy of meticulously planning things, closely evaluating and anticipating everything that could go right and wrong and then to see everything come together, like a glorious Orchestra in play, just the way the conductor envisioned it! It's like watching the final stroke of brush in a masterful painting. It's like planning the perfect bank heist! It feels like playing God! You know, whenever I hear people ``manifesting," it pisses me off but at the same time, I feel thankful to them. When I say "Manifest," I am talking about people who believe in manifestation, as imagined in the more popular sense - which is to simply and intensely think of what you desire and let the Universe do the rest of it. It's crazy how Tik Tok influencers ruin people with their Ali Express motivation. I will not deny that visualising and imagining in great detail what you wish to accomplish is an important aspect of achieving it. I am also not denying the role of an unknown force or let's say, luck, universe or whatever it is in making it happen. Gosh, when will I ever find a name for this strange thing? Let's call it "The Thing" for now. Anyway, there is a crucial link between the 2 that the Manifest tribe essentially miss - which is to plan and act on the plan. I shouldn't be complaining - I owe a lot to people who simply dream and not act. Let me explain using a curious phenomenon I observed when my city finally got its first Metro network after a painful wait. A very simple trick allowed me to get a Metro ticket within a minute as opposed to the 5-10 min average waiting queue for others. How? Ridiculously simple! When the modernity of Metro Railway arrived, it also came with new automated ticketing machines where one could purchase tickets without having to wait in a queue by simply inserting the right notes and coins. An experience totally new to the city used to the traditional long queues so nobody bothered to use these machines! The machines were there - for everyone to see - and use - yet nobody preferred to do it thus making my job easier!

And this became a recurring theme of my life. Whenever people made a big deal about any of my achievements, this is exactly how I felt about them. While I am not denying the fact that we wrote a great book with TGIO or the fact that tremendous effort had gone into the making of Annanymous t-shirts or in preparing for the TEDx talk, but I realised a lot of my success in these endeavours had to do with a very simple thing - I was either the only or first guy to be doing these things that nobody else bothered to. Only a small part of other people's reluctance had to do with infrastructural barriers that existed those days in terms of say publishing a book or starting up a business but the barrier for most people, as I observed, was simply mental! So I won half the game with the mind itself. This realisation also led to a deep sense of distrust towards people and it manifested in different ways. Politically, I had become far right because I felt that the politicians knew nothing about running the country and that nobody truly cared, and all the nation needed was a leader who genuinely wanted to do stuff for its people (Hint: Me). So I aspired to become the dictator of India someday! At home, I bullied everyone who questioned my life choices or for that matter gave any advice whatsoever even if they made sense. My mother was often a victim of this. The equation between us was appearing to change. I may have made her feel that I am now this grown-up intellectual with a better understanding of life and she may have started feeling that she is beginning to lose control over me but the truth is she was deeply in-charge of me in ways she wouldn't fully understand. She was the only person who had a strong hold over me. Even the most ridiculous things she said, I followed. For instance, one day, at the time of serving food, I happened to serve myself 2 servings and she insisted that I served myself a third one out of some age-old superstition she held about serving in odd numbers! In spite of being a rational grown-ass adult, I couldn't help myself from listening to her.

At work, be it TVF or during my stint at various student bodies, people found it difficult to work with me. At Annanymous, I was literally a one-man army running the entire show because I didn't trust anyone else to do the job as well. While I easily indulged with many women, I barely formed deep bonds with them - they were mostly lustful in nature. More significantly, I always thought the only difference between man and woman is the biology so I never quite grasped the nuances of what being a woman entails and treated them like I would treat men. So to say, as an animal, I was extremely successful. What do I mean by that? Well, there is a very important book/theory that helped me make sense of the world in a tremendous way actually. It didn't change my worldview or influence my life like some of the other books had but it played a huge role in providing an insight into human behaviour. The book, suggested by my friend Prashant Ghabak, is written by the renowned evolutionary biologist Richard Dawkins and is called the ***"Selfish Gene."*** This is the book that actually gave birth to the word "meme" - yet another early symbol of my later tryst with crypto' Yup, I am talking about all the memes we all share with each other every day. In this book, Dawkins talks about a very sagacious theory he calls the "Selfish Gene" theory. It provides a fascinating explanation for the guiding principle behind why most animals, including humans, behave the way they do and some of it may seem rather disturbing to the reader. The theory says that almost every action of all animals revolves around one central goal - to perpetuate one's genes forward. Simple! This is why bees sting even though they die after doing so in the larger interest of protecting the queen bee who bears eggs, the carrier of their genetic lineage! The reason a mother loves a child is not out of selflessness because she is wired to do so because by the programmer of this creation - the child carries her genes and is her tool to perpetuate her genetic imprint forward. Although mothers won't admit, they always have a favourite child, subconsciously the one they feel is most likely to carry their genes ahead. This also explains a lot of gender nuances in men and women.

Men, on the other hand, had no such gestation period. So, keeping in mind the subconscious programming to perpetuate their genes, they went on to inseminate as many women as possible. This explains so much of male and female behaviour today.

This also explains why men tend to cheat more because evolutionarily they always inseminated multiple women, thereby multiplying their genetic imprint. Men also tend to be more attracted to sports because they always hunted in a pack.

There were also many subtler ways this primal instinct manifested - for instance, I was extremely sensitive to any other life form, so even if the tiniest insect settled on my body, my wild survival reflexes would immediately want to shrug it off. So, from an animalistic standpoint, I had cracked the code on many aspects of how society functioned. While women offered themselves to me fully, I only used them for their bodies. I was a hardcore animal, a human animal.

As an animal, I also firmly believed that man is defined by his work, so I revolved my entire life around it. I felt that man is born to immerse himself in the activity of the world, climb up the human socio-hierarchical ladder, and then eventually die. So, my work and the legacy I wanted to leave behind became the priority of my life to the extent that I went about it like a horse with blinders on! I did not bother to care about what was happening around me - at home, whether the family needed me in any way, what my mother, father, and sister were going through, and if I could support them in any way - if not financially, at least emotionally. What the women I was with were seeking. None of it mattered. I was utterly and wholly consumed with my plans and animal like drive. One may have been fairly accurate in calling me selfish, I wanted to make the most of my life without having any complaints or regrets. So, in my 20s, I had planned out my life until the age of 30 in fair detail. What key things I wanted to achieve and how. I had also anticipated how all of them would be connected to each other even though they may have appeared disparate. I had adopted a specific strategy for my planning. Now, I feel there are roughly 2 kinds of life/career graphs, and I chose the second one. The first graph most people imagine, aspire to, or expect to look like is this, but they are usually wrong -

For all practical purposes, the first graph, for most people, looks like this:

The flat lines you see in each of these graphs are very crucial ones, and I like to call them B&D lines - Boredom and Death lines. This is when stagnancy seeps in, and more importantly, so does boredom, and it feels like the opposite of liveliness, which is essentially death. It may be no coincidence that even in a medical monitor, a flat line means death! People underestimate the role of boredom in their lives and in shaping human societies. I agree with the celebrated and fully self-taught Eric Hoffer who writes in his timeless classic *True Believer, Thoughts on the Nature of Mass Movements* that boredom is a key ingredient in the making of revolutions. Humans have immense propensity for drama! This is why I feel video games are dangerous, but more on that later. Every time boredom seeps in, humans look for change. So let's say the first B&D line in the graph denotes one's life in college. In college, one fairly knows the kind of life lay ahead - you know you are going to be stuck in a fairly predictable monotonous life for 3-4 years, so people keep themselves alive and entertained with aspirations and preparations for what they wish to do after college - in order to get out of their boredom - let's say they plan for their first job, and as soon as they land one, they have achieved their first reward, their first shot of vibrancy that makes them feel alive in the game. After spending some time in their first job, B&D seeps in again, so they keep themselves entertained with their next move, which is usually a jump in their career, so higher education becomes a natural tool for escape from boredom. They usually opt for their Masters or some sort of upskilling to move away from that B&D line. Consequently, reward arrives in the form of a more challenging and higher paying job. Then of course, B&D seeps in again, and it's time for the next big thing, which could be, let's say, a change of job. Then yet another B&D sets in even after a change of job, and then changing jobs no longer seem sustainable, so it's time to do something totally different - get married. With marriage comes another spike. The early excitement of newfound companionship fades, then B&D seeps in again, and so they plan to have a kid, which leads to another spike and newfound excitement arrives in the relationship. Then once the child grows to a certain age, a stagnancy of a stronger kind comes in, and this time, clueless about where the next shot of liveliness will come from, they settle for a desperate makeshift arrangement, let's say a promotion at work, and after this is when the most potent and meanest B&D of their life hits them - mid-life crisis. By this time, they feel stuck in their marriage, and with the daunting reality that they have to spend the rest of their lives with the same person. Their ability to take risks becomes zero because their family is dependent on them. There are only 2 ways to deal with this - make radical choices - like resorting to spiritual/religious solace, or indulge in the thrill of secretly having an affair with a new partner, etc. The second and most common choice is to come to terms with your life, which is usually accompanied with resentment, regret & bitterness.

The pros to such a life are:

1. It's safe, low risk, and has a higher sense of socio-financial security. You may not have excess money, but there is at least always enough money to lead a decent and dignified life.

2. Goals such as attaining a Masters, a new job, or a work promotion are much more realistic to achieve, so a way out of boredom is pretty much within reach.

3. There is little resistance from society, and social validation and support largely come easy.

The cons of such a life graph are -

The B&D lines exceed those of liveliness, which means they spend more life in boredom than in the thrill of living.

The biggest con, according to me, is that such a life is largely driven by goals of other members of society and they do not come from the place of personal and individual expression. So they all tend to have standard goals: first job, higher education, promotion, marriage, children, etc. Only when the mid-life crisis hits do they realise that following others may not have worked for them, and by the time realisation dawns, it's too late. Resentment usually is attributed to others - either parents, the spouse, the society, etc.

Of course, this may not hold true for everyone with such a life; I am just sharing an overarching observation.

Now, the graph that I choose for myself is this:

The cons for such a life are:

High risk. As goals can be ambitious and seemingly impractical, chances of failing are much higher than in graph 1, so rewards aren't always assured.

You need progressively bigger challenges to tackle. Once a challenge is tackled, the next one needs to be bigger. For example, for someone who has founded a successful start-up, to move out of his B&D line, he needs to find something more challenging to solve. Falling back could lead to a major existential crisis.

The rewards come in late if they do. So while people in graph 1 have a constant and early inflow of financial reward, people in graph 2 may have to wait longer, and even then, it isn't assured.

Social support and validation may be minimal, sometimes even to the extent of isolation.

Pros:

While it is true that if successful, the rewards come in late, but when they come, they are usually exponentially high. Let's take the example of a farsighted entrepreneur who has been running an AR/VR company, putting back all the money he earns into the business, overall running losses for over 5 years and barely making any money for himself. Then one day, Silicon Valley goes berserk about Metaverse, and his company is acquired for half a billion dollars, and he becomes a millionaire seemingly overnight! He made more money in one year than people in graph 1 will make in their entire life.

There is always much more thrill than boredom. Because the goals are usually unique, the solutions to those problems also require unique approaches, thereby keeping the brain cells sufficiently exercised and entertained. So there are always micro wins and losses which make life very exciting.

The sense of resentment, bitterness, and guilt is much less. As personal desires have largely found expression and goals have been designed around personal ambitions, and decision-making revolves around self, with little influence or consideration for anyone else, the chances of resentment, even during failures, are low.

If successful, social acceptance comes in the form of idolising or even worship!

Now, all these intellectually sophisticated graphs and plans went for a toss that morning when I woke up with the book under my pillow - like a house that is up for cleaning during the festive season. Bags of junk thrown out!

After my mother finally revealed hidden details from my childhood, I acknowledged something strange was happening to me. It also became clear that it could not be explained by any source I had resorted to for answers until then. I would have to look in a completely new direction, to a completely new source.

It seems when I was 3 years of age, as was the routine for me those days, I was operating the VCR machine and watching my favourite cartoon or movie. When my mother called me from the kitchen, I did not respond. So she called for me again, and I failed to respond once again. Anxious, she ran out of the kitchen and came to the room to see me sitting still but unresponsive. She was now beginning to panic with her mind and heart rate running amok, her motherly instincts concerned for her child's well-being gripped her as she slowly inched towards me and then gently moved me with her hands. I fell, dropped on the floor in the same posture. Still unresponsive. Shocked and stunned by what was clearly her life's most terrifying moment, she froze! Not knowing what to do in a foreign land, she immediately dialled my father who then rushed me to the hospital. After an EEG test, I was "diagnosed" with "Epilepsy" - a neurological disorder marked by sudden recurrent episodes of sensory disturbance, loss of consciousness, or convulsions, associated with abnormal electrical activity in the brain.

It seems similar episodes repeated 2-3 times until the age of 4, and then they stopped, but the medication continued for much longer. When I heard this, I smiled and I told my mom, "I don't think it was what you think it is." She had no clue what I was saying, and I didn't want to speak further, so I just stopped at that. I returned from my talk that night, a man at much more ease, not in search of anything. A strange kind of poise. That night itself, I went out for a round of drinks with 2 friends, one a Protestant Catholic and the other, a Hindu by birth but an atheist, a close childhood friend, a charming and witty boy who had grown-up to become a boring adult. He is a classic example of what the system can do to wonderful people. It just sucked the life out of him. So I am sitting with these guys, and the most unlikely topic of conversation for Mumbai-bred young men is God & Religion. There is so much running around for survival that is deeply entrenched in us that there is hardly time for God in it in daily lives. But I kid you not, that night is still so vivid in my memory. We spoke for 3 hours. In fact, I spoke for 3 hours straight, like a school teacher explaining her curious infancy pupils, I spoke in great detail about God, Religion, and Spirituality! How? Don't ask. Just get used to it from now on. So what did I tell them really? Let me tell you as well. Everything I told them. Let's assume some of the Physicist's proposition that the world is indeed unreal then is there anyone who managed to get out of this unreal world and wake up to reality? Yes, there are many people but a few popular ones are Jesus, Mohammed, Buddha among others, and they may be called Enlightened beings or also known as the Awakened Ones for they have awakened to who they really are outside this created virtual reality - outside this dream. It is impossible to miss such a being, and maybe this is why when someone got enlightened, they naturally drew a lot of attention from those around them, and people worshipped them and formed a religion around them? Is it possible because they have awakened themselves in the virtual world, they have managed to hack the game completely and so it is possible that they could perform "miracles" that defy the rules of the game, such as walking on Water, turning blood into wine etc? Then I got asked why don't they do it often and baffle everyone? Well, let's take the example of a toddler and a grown adult. For an adult, to move a chair is an easy task, but for a toddler it is a superhuman ability so will the adult keep pulling the chair just so he can prove his prowess to the child? No. The adult fully knows that when the child grows he too can move the chair like he does, and it is beyond him to flaunt to an infant child. Similarly, Enlightened beings, with their elevated consciousness see everyone else as their children too so it is beyond them to perform tricks to their children with the intention of flexing! They are also embarrassed by any form of worship because it is not a great deal. Anyone who grows up can get there too. It's like the Metro ticket analogy again - just not in the context of ticket or business but in the context of life as a whole. Enlightenment is available for everyone, but the vast majority are simply lost in the games of this unreal world so naturally to those few who seek, it becomes available and others make a big deal out of it. Is this the reason why every Indian household at least once has heard the old adage *Jeevan maya hai,* (life is an illusion). Was the ancient Indian civilisation privy to this realisation as well? Now the billion-dollar question really is - how to get enlightened? How to experience the world beyond this illusionary reality? To address this, I am going to tell you a very brief story of some Enlightened beings, and the answer will naturally come from you.

The first story is of a very beautiful being. His presence was so full of affection that if he entered a conference full of Wall Street Executives even today, wearing his characteristic white robes, all those suited men would be cluelessly drawn to him - I am of course talking about one of history's most enduring mysteries - Jesus Christ. I am in fact going to share with you an open secret from Spiritual circles in India. Jesus actually died in Kashmir, and this is how it all transpired concealed from the ears of popular history. There are 2 big mysteries in religion. The first one is called the "Unknown Years of Jesus" and the second one is the "Resurrection of Jesus." For someone who is perhaps the most discussed and documented man in history, nobody really knows where Jesus was between the ages 13-29. Can you believe it? It is only known that he disappeared from Jerusalem to an unknown location at the age of 13 and returned only once he turned 30! These years are referred to by historians as the "Unknown years of Jesus." This has been a subject of countless conspiracy theories in the world with everyone having an opinion as to where Jesus was in those missing years, but in Indian spiritual circles, everyone just knows what happened. There is an enchanting chapter in the Bible called "The Gift of Magi" that chronicles a rather strange event. As soon as Jesus was born, it seems "Three Wise Men" are said to have appeared from the Eastern world, following the stars, and offering gifts to the newly born Jesus. Technically, this was to be the first-ever Christmas present and is the genesis of the tradition of Gifting during Christmas. My guess is, this could also be the origin of "Secret Santa" as the identity of these Three Men was never known. Nothing more has ever been written or known in the Bible about these mysterious men. Now, the Indian legend goes like this - in the Buddhist tradition, their leader, the Dalai Lama, is appointed at birth after following the stars. These 3 wise men were essentially Buddhist monks from India who landed in Jerusalem, following the stars as prescribed in their religion, and secretly anointed Jesus as their next Dalai Lama. After the age of 13, Jesus moved to India where after years of intense training in ancient Hindu and Buddhist Meditation techniques, he became the absolute Master of the Mystical Science of Yoga. His control over his own body and mind was so phenomenal that it was widely known and accepted that Jesus was a rare being, a Yogi of the highest order. There is a very simple litmus test to ascertain this. In Yoga, there is a particular suspended state of consciousness (known as Samadhi in Yogic parlance) called the *Nirvikalpa Samadhi*. Now largely, there are 2 kinds of samadhis. One - in which you experience altered states of consciousness and trance by very much retaining your body consciousness. This is a relatively easier feat to achieve. Then there are states that are so intense and deep that it becomes difficult to retain body consciousness so the body is dropped causing "death" as we know it. Then there is a third state which requires mastery of the highest order. If I have to use an analogy to explain this then imagine a man either having sex or pleasing himself. Early on in the process of this pleasure, it is easy for him to resist ejaculation, he can continue experiencing a sense of pleasure without the climax of ejaculation around the corner. Now, as he pleases himself further, the pleasure grows stronger and stronger and it reaches the point of peak sexual pleasure where he has momentarily lost sensory control and an ejaculation of vital semen is inevitable. What if one could experience that peak pleasure while he regains full control and is also able to resist ejaculation? This analogy is both figurative and literal. Literal because it is an actual tantric practice where a man climaxes and experiences peak sexual pleasure but with a twist. By assuming a particular posture (Asana in Yogic dictionary), he manages to "in" jaculate which is similar to ejaculation but with the semen being retained within. Like Steve Jobs learnt in India. The example is figurative because while the pleasure of and conditions to attain a samadhi state and that of sexual states are not comparable. The analogy I wanted to draw is, Nirvikalpa Samadhi is a state where one experiences hypnotic states that are impossible to experience without leaving the body but at the same time your control over your body and mind is so perfect that you retain body consciousness at the same time. It's an unimaginable feat, but Jesus is said to have perfected it. Now at the age of 30, he returns back to Jerusalem and then of course when a man with as radical a realisation and mastery as him arrives anywhere, he attracts attention of all kinds.

They then took his body down, wrapped it in linen cloth and covered it in spices as was the burial tradition those days, and enclosed his tomb with a rolling stone.

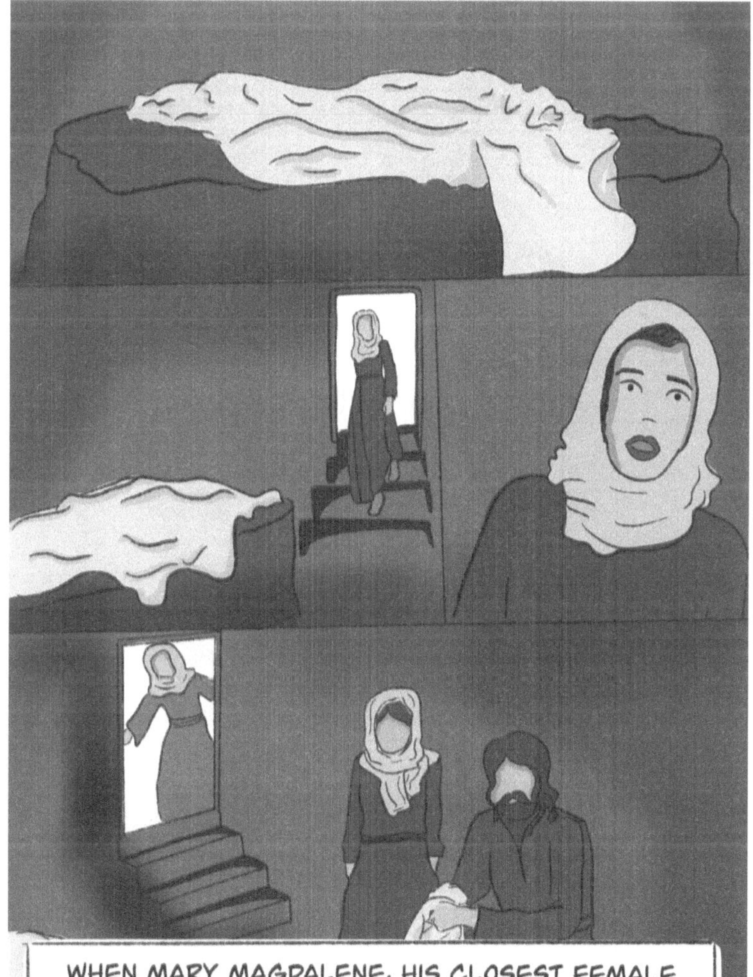

Confused and anxious, when she looked outside the tomb, she saw someone who she first identified as a gardener. When the gardener came close, Mary couldn't believe her eyes; it was Jesus himself!

Over the next few days, Jesus would present himself to his closest disciples. One of them was Saint Thomas, who refused to acknowledge his Master. This became the origin for the phrase "Doubting Tom." In order to dispel his disciples' doubt, Jesus held Thomas's hand and placed it on his wound, and when he felt Jesus' blood on his hand, only then could Thomas believe what he was witnessing. How could this miracle take place? Looks like there is a rational explanation for this seemingly inexplicable phenomenon. The Yogis know what exactly transpired. While on the cross, Jesus had attained to Nirvikalpa Samadhi, a state in which body processes are consciously slowed down to such an extent that people assume they are dead. His resurrection was nothing but a coming out of the samadhi state and regaining full body consciousness. Now, such an occurrence may have happened for the first time in that region so understandably, it became a huge deal and overwhelmed people for a long time. After his resurrection, Jesus instructed his disciples to carry his message across different regions, and then there is no account of where Jesus went after that. Some say he went to Spain, some say he ascended to heaven. Indian Yogis too have an account of that! Now, what is well-known and documented is that St Thomas (Yup, the same Doubting Tom), one of Jesus's 12 direct disciples, known as the Apostles, did arrive in India to spread his Master's message. He was, as the Christians say, martyred by locals in what is today known as the Southern city of Chennai where his tomb lies even today. So contrary to popular belief, Christianity is as old in India as Christ himself! Now, what is not popularly recorded in history is that St Thomas did not travel to India alone; he had company - he was accompanied by his Master Jesus Christ himself who is said to have spent his last few years in the mortal body in what is today Kashmir. Even now there is a tomb of a mysterious figure in the heart of Kashmir that locals call Yuza Asaf, who as per ancient records that exist even today, describe the tomb to be of a Prophet from the West, who the locals confirm to be Jesus Christ. The feet of the tomb carry a nail mark. While there are other accounts in Spiritual circles as to where Jesus actually left his body in Kashmir, the consensus is largely that he very much spent the last years of his life in Kashmir. If you are interested in pursuing this story further, I would recommend 2 well-documented sources - a BBC Documentary called Jesus in Kashmir and a movie called *The Man from Earth*.

The second story is one of the most endearing and profound stories a man has ever lived. His story in many ways is the most classic spiritual journey of all-time - one that of a Spiritual frontbencher. Just before his birth, as was the tradition in royal families those days, a holy man was invited to pay a visit and bless the soon-to-be born child and during that visit, a prediction was made that would impact the child's upbringing in a big way. The holy man made an ambivalent prophecy that the child would either grow up to be a great emperor or a great saint. The father trembled at the possibility of his child turning out to be anything but a king as himself.

She died soon after giving birth to the child. Fully aware and cautious of the prediction about the child, the father did everything to shield the boy from harsh realities of life, should it trigger an iota of spiritual sentiment within his son. So, the child spent most of his childhood and early adulthood within the corridors of his palace with unbridled access to indulgences of all kinds. He would later marry his cousin and give birth to a son named Rahula.

Everyone he loved and cherished, including himself, would die one day. This daunting realisation of transience was enough to instil deep within him an acute sense of curious urge to explore the mysteries of life. Nobody knew what was brewing within him, but they would all eventually learn it the hard way - one day, as he could no longer contain his spirit of inquiry, he simply ran away from the palace to never return the same man again. With a maddening sense of commitment to crack this game of life, he went to countless Indian teachers at the time. It was widely established wherever he went that he was prodigal, a rare student, with gifted capabilities who many teachers gladly offered their own position to, thereby hoping to relieve themselves, but he had no such interest, demonstrating a sense of spiritual virtuousness and integrity very rare among spiritual seekers. He was possessed by a pain so unbearable yet sweet I hope that every human goes through someday. People think what happened to this man on that fateful full moon day in the future would be the most significant day of his life, but most people don't understand and appreciate the bittersweet pain of the journey. He hopped from one school to another, mastering all known techniques of the time, but yet the real deal still was at bay. How does one know? One always knows. The real deal is so phenomenal that it is impossible to miss. So, when it still hadn't happened, he chose to put himself through extreme torture - the kind I doubt many modern-day men are capable of. He chose to wander through the wilderness and only eat if something was offered to him. That beautiful man was reduced to skin and bones, still carrying an elegance of a different kind. Then at some point, trying itself became a burden, so he came up with a much simpler plan. A do-or-die plan in the most literal sense. He found a tree in the forest under which he would simply sit, but under a powerful vow. The plan was simple, he sits there until it happens or he perishes.

OVER 40 DAYS OR SO, HE BATTLED THE DEMON MARA WHO
TRIED TO LURE HIM OUT OF HIS VOW WITH TEMPTATION OF
ALL KIND

THEN ON THAT BEAUTIFUL FULL MOON DAY, IT
HAPPENED AND THE WORLD RECEIVED THE FORTUNE
OF A MASTER OF PHENOMENAL COMPASSION AND
COMPETENCE

Thus, Gautama became The Buddha. It is said that The Buddha was born, got enlightened, and died on the same day (different years, of course). The particular full moon day later came to be named after him and is called Buddha Purnima in India.

Regarding Mohammed too, as I mentioned previously, he spent 40 days meditating in a cave and came out reciting something of beautiful aesthetics which later became Gospel truth, the Holy Quran for his followers.

So, is there a technology that can get us out of this illusory world without having to insert a chip in our brain or going to Elon Musk? A technology that is available to everyone irrespective of the language they speak, the amount of money they have, or the geography they reside in? Yes, Yoga & Meditation are eternal technologies that the creator has tastefully and sublimely crafted and made available to everyone in order to get out of this creation. The Control Panel for this game of life exists - not at any hidden external place - it exists within each one of us to hack.

Amongst all the phases of my life, if I was to pick one to re-live, uff, it will have to be this. It felt like a lover being reunited with his love after a brief separation, a young soldier with his wife, a lost child with his mother, a lost pet with their Master. Over the next 3 months, I fully immersed myself reading about this new realm I had entered and its beautiful mysterious residents. The story of their lives, like poetry to my curious parched soul. Their eyes were portals, their body, temples, their words, like cosmic melody! Love, Anticipation, and more Love!

When the Saints Go Marching In

During my days in school, we had a breakthrough annual day one year. It wasn't the regular affair - the school was organising a musical for the first time, in an auditorium outside the school. There was a huge fanfare around it. There were paid tickets to attend the show which was quite unusual for any school function in India in the 90s! I was part of a special dance called the Skeleton Dance. As the name suggests, the dancers would all adorn a special Skeleton costume that would glow in the dark in the presence of neon lights (In the 90s, a lot of kids in Africa and India wouldn't even need a costume to pull this off 😳). A rather unique song was chosen for this unique dance - an old Christian hymn called "When The Saints Go Marching In," the most popular version of which is by Louis Armstrong (is there any song that Louis Armstrong has sung and is not the most popular version of that song?) but my favourite version is the duet Armstrong had with Danny Kaye. Even after the show was over, I sang this song anywhere and everywhere I went, so much so that it became a huge hit even among my cousins. It almost feels like a personal obligation that whenever I discover something significant, I must share it with the entire world! But it would take me a decade and a half to truly understand what the song really meant. There are 2 particular stanzas in the song -

Oh, when the Saints Go Marching In
Oh, when the Saints Go Marching In,
I want to be in that number.
When the Saints Go Marching In.

Oh when the New World is Revealed.
Oh, when the New World is revealed,
I want to be in that number.
When the New World is Revealed.

It is my deep desire and wish that everyone goes through this phase in their life. In Spiritual Parlance, it may be called awakening, not fully awakened - That would mean becoming The Buddha - An enlightened being - awakening means the start of the process to a new world, a new possibility. Why did I live in separation with these people for so long? The joy of reunion, the fulfilment of a pained lover. Uff!

I read about them - the Enlightened beings - day and night and still longed for more. It's one of my greatest privileges to be acquainting you with them as I shall do more elaborately in Vol 2. You will be surprised how strange life can be. A few notable mentions I would like to make in this Volume-

Osho

If Buddha was a Spiritual frontbencher, then Osho was clearly a backbencher. By his own admission, he was a Spiritual Rebel, a Spiritual Playboy. All Spiritual people are by nature rebels, and to be a rebel among rebels must say something about the man! My experience of Osho was very different from what he was pretending to be. I knew he was putting up a show and man, everyone fell for it and how! Reading Osho's Autobiography is one of my life's most intimate experiences. Osho's Enlightenment story is quirky, much like the man himself. After years of intense sadhana that everyone around him was privy to, one day he became hopeless. Hopeless not in the sense of losing any hope of getting enlightened but in some way, he stopped hoping for it to happen. Much to the surprise and bafflement of everyone around him, one day, he insisted on having beer for the first time in his life. As with Buddha and every other seeker, trying becomes a liability beyond a point so they just rebel against everything they have been trying towards all their life. This man has some beer and one night he sneaks to a nearby garden, seated under a tree pretty much deep into the intoxication of the night.

After some time, the security guard hears a loud laughter and, alarmed, he goes inside the garden to inspect. There, below the tree, sat not a man but an all-encompassing force. It had finally happened to Him. His Game was over. At the age of 21! Twenty freakin one! At this point, I had no clue what Enlightenment is and why Osho would laugh but I imagined it to be something very phenomenal. What must it be?

After his Enlightenment, Osho became a professor of Philosophy at a nearby University. Every month on the day of salary distribution, Osho never went to receive it himself. He always picked a student from his class to go and collect it on his behalf. The instruction was clear - The student was free to keep any money they wished for themselves, even the whole if they desired, and pass on the remaining to Osho. He would never count how much money he received but it so happened that never during his entire stint as a professor did any student choose to keep even a penny for themselves. This is Osho, at his truest but sadly, people have largely fallen for his act.

In Tibet for thousands of years, a certain sect has tried to preserve a unique set of 99 bodies in which some extraordinary things happened. You can call it a private museum or a mystical lab of sorts. Because events that have happened to those bodies don't happen again and again, and definitely not easily, they were preserved. There are bodies there in which someone's third eye opened with such a tremendous force that it broke a hole!

Body number 97 in this collection is of Osho from a previous time, a previous drama. Every Master leaves behind a unique legacy, Buddha for instance, left behind a living spiritual process that has now lasted for over 2500 years which is unprecedented. In the material context, it could be like building a Google, which only Stanford frontbenchers like Larry Page and Sergie Brin were capable of. Similarly, only a Spiritual frontbencher as Buddha could create something that could actively last for over 2 and a half millennia! Osho's legacy for me has been his words. The man speaks with a clarity, potency, and charm that can move even the hardest of sceptics!

When the popular Netflix documentary, Wild Country, was released, that sight when Osho appears on screen for the first time is so vivid in my memory even today. A glorious man, with a flower-like presence, a wickedly endearing smile. There were tears rolling down uncontrollably. It was one of the most beautiful moments of my life but it wasn't the first time it happened. Technically, it was the third and all of them happened in this very beautiful phase for very similar reasons - reasons I did not know. The first 2 were for Ramana Maharishi and Jiddu Krishnamurthi, about whom we will discuss later in Vol 2. I had never seen or heard about these people in my life but here I was shedding tears of joy just at the sight of them!

Meher Baba

Meher Baba's father was an intense spiritual seeker in Persia who one day attempted a severe form of spiritual practice in his youth by drawing a circle on Earth and sitting inside it without food and water for 40 days. Unable to continue, after 30 days he came out, drank some water from a nearby lake, and fell flat on the ground. He was later awakened by a voice that said, "That which you long for, you will receive only through your son." Not having any intention to marry before this, he now married a Persian woman and later moved to Pune, India. Merwan Sheriar Irani would be his second son. Merwan had a largely regular childhood. When he turned 19, as on any other day, he was on his way home from school and while crossing a tree, a strange woman called Hazrat Babajan called to him. Hazrat Babajan belonged to a Royal Afghan Family and she literally ran away from home on the day of her wedding, travelling all over in search of Spiritual guidance and would eventually get enlightened in India at the age of 37 after much struggle. She had made this particular tree in Pune her abode and watched Merwan pass by every day.

For 9 months, he simply lay on his bed, gazing at the roof. While his mother sought medical intervention, his father knew very well what was happening. Merwan would later go on to become Meher Baba, an

Enlightened Master. One day, I was at a friend's place for a party, and one particular song that played zapped me like a bolt. I vividly recollected the strange sound at the start of the song to be the sound I was experiencing from my supposed Epileptic episode at the age of 3. On further research, it turned out that the song titled Baba O'Riley by The Who was a tribute to Meher Baba by the band.

My life has now become a living videogame. I was now part of a Cosmic Treasure hunt, the end reward of the game being Enlightenment! Where do I find my next clue? I made a list of all those places I need to visit soon: Jesus' tomb in Kashmir, Osho's ashram in Pune, Ramana Maharishi's ashram in Tiruvannamalai, Hazarat Babjan's tomb, Meher Baba's Tomb, and every other place with which and person with whom I seemed to have some strange connection. I had no clue how I was going to be able to set on this important journey spanning across geographically diverse regions, but I knew this is the single most important thing in my life right now - my next clue. I know this may sound ridiculous, maybe even borderline fanatical, but how to explain what was happening within me? I actually tried to find the Excel Sheet I had prepared for this journey to share with you, but I couldn't. It should be there somewhere. I went to sleep that night determined to plan and arrange for resources the following morning. How would I convince my mom to set me on this journey? I didn't know. Maybe tell her the truth? With these pointers, I went to sleep and woke up to a text message from a friend in Manhattan, New York, Apurva. It was an invite for her wedding a month or 2 away then. The wedding was being conducted in Pune, where lies Osho's Ashram, Hazrat Babjan's tomb, and just a few miles away, also Meher Baba's Tomb. I see what "The Thing" was up to here. But the absolute Masterstroke of "The Thing" was the timing - Looks like Apurva is getting married on my birthday! Sweet timing. It confirmed what I had a sneaky feeling about since "The awakening" - that my 28th year and 35th year will be significant years of my life.

I am now a step closer to my next clue - a critical one. It will either come at Osho's ashram, Hazrat Babajan's Tomb, or Meher Baba's Tomb, or maybe all of them? I don't know, but what I did know is that an exciting gift awaits me this coming birthday. What is it going to be?

After a patient wait brimming with anticipation, the day of reckoning had finally arrived. What did "The Thing" have in store for me? How will the next clue be unveiled to me? Will Osho show up from his tomb? Will Meher Baba show up like a translucent, ghost-like figure as they show in the movies? God-damn it, can someone freaking fast forward this day already? I really want to know how this is going to pan out. Where is the 2x speed button for life? How can I fast forward this? Now, another woman enters my life, and we all know what this usually means....

Please scan this code to unlock $GIC tokens and
Bonus content for this chapter

Question 6 -

Ponder and introspect about this in solitude - you don't have to write your answer now - you may write only once you feel ready to write and whenever that is, you will write honestly what comes to you and nothing else.

When you think about yourself . When you say "I" who are you referring to - Is it your body? Then why do you call it "your body" and not You? Is it the name? Then why is it "My name" and not Me? Is it your mind? Is it your personality?

Are you - a silent, constant, persistent voice that has remained unchanged, unmoving and exactly the same from the time you were born till now witnessing everything or are you that ever changing self that would be different if you born in another country, or if those incidents didn't happen to you in your childhood, and if you were born to different parents - the self that is temporary and subject to change?

Chapter 07

When the New World is Revealed

Imagine you wake up one day to a new world.
Would you be scared? Excited? Confused?
Immersed, lost perhaps?
Come, let's figure out together…

The plan was to arrive in Pune early in the morning - first visit Osho's ashram then head to Meher Baba's Tomb and then, if feasible, Hazrat Babjan's tomb before rushing to the wedding festivities. I leave home and as planned first arrive in Pune - a city with pleasant weather, a traditional Marathi undercurrent I like but this visit is not about Pune - I am on a mission for my next clue so I head straight to Osho ashram, situated in the posh locality of Koregaon Park in the city. As I reach the place, it doesn't quite match with my impression of an ashram - with its towering walls and an unusually high number of security guards, the place clearly resembles a fortress more than an ashram. As I enquired my way inside the ashram, I was in for a rude shock - the entry fee is a staggering INR 3500/- which was more than my budget for this entire trip! I had read somewhere that after Osho left the body, all his assets including his talks, ashram etc were usurped by a bunch of businessmen in Switzerland who had no interest or idea of the Master's teachings. I don't know for a fact - maybe they are his devotees too. "How could Osho allow this to happen? What have they done of this Beautiful Master's legacy?" I wondered. This was one of my life's most disappointing anti-climaxes. Forget about Osho waking up from his tomb, I couldn't even get past the gates of his ashram. Dejected, I left the place quickly towards my next destination - Meher Baba's Tomb in Meherabad (the township in the city of Ahmednagar named after Him and owned by His trust), 72 miles from Pune. Still reeling from the sadness of not being able to visit Osho's tomb, at the same time, reeling with curiosity on what awaits me next in this Treasure Hunt, I arrive at Ahmednagar from where Meherabad is a 15 mins ride. As I inch closer to Meherabad, a sense of familiarity overwhelms me. A smile breaks out as if going to visit my own after a long time. The neighbourhood is tranquil, sparsely populated just as I would hope an ideal Spiritual place to be. As I inch closer to his tomb, the already scarce number of people reduce further. I am dropped right outside His tomb and looks like I am legit the only person in this whole place! I Love You Baba! I screamed within me in elation. He made himself available to me for a one on one meeting . How kind of you! I enter his tomb on which is engraved in bold words "I Have Come Not To Teach But To Awaken." In that moment, like Zap , I found an answer to everything that was happening to me in the last few months.

"Oh Baba, it was you all along!" How could I have not known? I gasped in relief and gratitude. You see, Spiritual growth is a delicate process and it is no surprise that a lot of people found in Asylums end up there as a result of misdirected spiritual practices. I thought my transformation in the last few months was purely psychological but turns out it was hardly that. In that moment in the tomb, I realised everything that had happened. My transition from my former ignorant sleep state to my current awakening state was beautifully planned and executed. I mean, absolutely brilliant! The pace at which I transitioned between states, it is easy for anyone to go crazy but my Kundalini (don't fret about what terms like these mean rn, I will make you a geek on these aspects in Vol 2) was managed insanely well. And remember my NoFap state? Oh well, that was just a trick to keep my pranas stable so that He could do His work without any disturbance and with absolute precision.

I was just being played! Oh gosh. Never thought I would gush in love at the prospect of being played by someone! Not knowing what to do next, I sat there for some time trying to meditate. LOL. Looks like not much had changed as far as my ability to sit still and meditate since my Vipassana days. Plus, I was also wearing denim which made it even more difficult to sit so after a few minutes of embarrassing myself in front of Him, I left. Equipped with fresh knowledge and insight but still waiting for my next cue. Heading back to Pune, unsure whether I had the time to stop by Hazrat Babjan's tomb before heading towards the wedding, I cramped myself into a crowded vehicle headed towards Pune. From my years of travel, this was now a familiar experience for me. Like a lot of Indians, I had learnt to adjust myself into a vehicle designed to accommodate 5 people but even the engineers may not know this secret - that car can actually accommodate 15. India is clearly not for beginners. In this crowded mess, my phone vibrates, by the time I squeeze my hand through the human maze to finally reach my pocket, I miss the call. It was V's call. By now, you should anticipate a major shift in my story, the moment a woman arrives. It is a recurrent theme. They come, I transition, and they leave as if it was all they were there for.

V reached out to me after watching my TEDx talk. This was during my "animal" days. She lost her father early on and grew up to successfully complete her formal training as a dentist. During our initial days, she kept insisting that I enrolled for this Yoga programme offered by her Guru. I was still in my pre-awakening days then so I sternly told her that I had no interest in her Guru or in any programme offered by him. She understood and simply told me "You will go really far one day." I thought it was in the context of my TEDx talk. Now, women are phenomenal actors! Right from faking an orgasm to concealing a gamut of emotional undercurrents perfectly without an iota of external appearance. But one thing a woman can never conceal is her feelings for a man she truly loves. I knew V was madly in love with me. She also sent me an Annanymous love note on my website expecting me to not know! I know everything. Taking advantage of her love for me, I exploited it for lustful gains. "I have never been with anyone before and I promised myself if I get intimate with someone, that person would be the first and last" she told me with a compelling force. She was right, she later got initiated into monkhood by the same Guru she kept talking to me about. But not before doing her bit in my life.

V called me that day on my way from Meher Baba's samadhi to offer me a gift. I don't think she knew it was my birthday but the timing of it was magical. It seems V's Guru was to be in Mumbai a few days later as part of a public conversation with a very popular Bollywood director and she wanted me to attend it. The event was to be held in an upscale auditorium and even the most economical pass would cost around INR 3K but V, being a volunteer in the Guru's ashram, had arranged a free pass for me. She had no idea of my current awakening. Not even an inkling of an idea but somehow here she was calling me on my birthday, to gift me a pass so that I could be in her Guru's presence. With times being very different from when we first met, I accepted her gift with immense gratitude. I had received my next clue. I decided to head straight to the wedding and then rush to Mumbai.

The day of the event arrived. I have been a huge admirer of this particular Bollywood director and was perhaps the first time I was to see him outside the borders of a screen but this visit was clearly not about him. Not knowing what to expect from the event, I arrived at the venue, pleasantly greeted by volunteers. I am guided to my designated seating area just a tier behind the VIP/Top tier seating. As the fully packed auditorium eagerly awaits for the commencement of the event, there is soothing music filling up the ambience of the hall. Beautiful! Soon, the director walks into the stage first then follows the Guru and in an unprecedented moment, my body stands up and there are tears rolling down my face. I had never experienced anything like this for any living person in my entire life before. Not wanting anyone around to see me like this, I quickly wipe my tears and gear up for the conversation. There were 2 highlights from the entire conversation. The first one was when this particular fool stood up to ask him a question. I call that guy a fool because his question reeked of insincerity. How do I know? I just know it. Firstly, if you have a chance to ask a freaking enlightened being a question, then it better be something that is eating you up. The irony however is, if you possess a question that burns you so intensely then the answer simply arrives, without you having to ask it on a mic! This fool stood up to ask a question of much profundity with such callousness, I felt he deserved a slap. His question, I found much more ridiculous than himself - quoting a very popular, revered and chronicled Master - Disciple duo from the Indian lore who we shall for now refer to as K and A respectively, this guy asks the Guru, how could he become the A to the K that the Guru is or in other words - the perfect disciple to him. I found this question very fascinating. If you had a choice between wanting to be like K and A, why on Earth would you ask the Guru to make you like A and not K? People love to worship - to be enslaved but not empowered. But I was barely surprised, this fool looked like the kind of idiot who would rather spend his life asking questions and not y be empowered enough to answer for himself.

The other highlight from the event was the Guru's core teaching. He had a very interesting approach - one that did not involve reading or following any written or spoken lessons of which I was certainly apprehensive then. His core teaching revolved around the science and technique of Yoga. As simple as that! A few simple Yogic Technologies - If one finds answers with these techniques he has to offer, then well and good! if it doesn't work then one is just free to part ways. By now, I was well aware of what Yoga as a science really means and facilitates and after Vipassana, this is the first time I felt encouraged to actually give it a shot.

So, as soon as I went home, I looked up upcoming programmes from the Guru's foundation. As luck may have it, there is one happening the following week - at a centre walking distance from my house in Mumbai! How cool is that! It's as if the programme came walking to me. As I tried to register, the payment failed. I tried again, it failed yet again. So close to learning this new technique yet so far! Is this the one going to get me out of this illusory world? Is this going to be the final chapter of an unfinished business? Disappointed and irritated at the payment gateway, I shut my laptop hoping to register the following day. Next day, as I inch closer to the registration, a pop-up appears. It seems the Guru is going to be physically present in Bangalore next month where he will directly be offering the practice to all the participants - something that happens only rarely. By now, months of so-called Spiritual madness had gripped me and in my single pointed commitment to unravel what was happening, I ignored everything else. My savings were fully exhausted s in these months of travel and exploration. I was in no mood to do or think of anything else until I had some satisfactory redressal. I borrowed money from my sister(I'm a proud feminist you see 😊) to enrol for the programme in Bangalore. With a month to go, I started preparing my own way, from what I had grasped until then. There were 2 songs that were constant companions through this phase. The first one is, popularly known as Om Namah Shivaya by Bob Marley. The voice and rendition is so hypnotic that I could listen to it all day and I did! I started looking at Bob Marley in a totally different light. Only after some research, I found out that the song is wrongly attributed to Bob Marley but was composed and sung by an American guy named Krishna Das and a sweet coincidence was that we shared the same birthday. There is an interesting story about how Krishna Das came to offer Hindu devotional music, known as Kirtan. One day he was sitting in the presence of his Master, Neem Karoli Baba, who was the same Master Steve Jobs came looking for in India. A random thought popped into his mind - a thought to offer

Hindu devotional music, a phenomenon totally unheard of for a White American man. Confused, he ignored the thought. Then it came to his awareness again and this time his eyes met with that of his Master who smiled and acknowledged this thought after which he took up the service full time. Today Krishna Das is one of the most popular and certainly, divine Kirtankars in the world. Along with listening to this song, I also retained my semen, avoided alcohol and cigarettes. The second song, we shall discuss soon.

I arrived at the venue in Bangalore with roughly 4000 participants. I am sorry but I couldn't stop feeling livid at the kind of people who were coming in. With this new phase, I started having zero tolerance for bullshit. I can see through people's bullshit so easily, bloody idiots. We shall understand the technicalities of why this was happening later and why I may be appearing so brash to you suddenly. All these fools bring these fancy Yoga mats, freshly purchased Yoga pants from Amazon, but leave their brains and sincerity behind. People think the first thing they need in order to receive Yoga is a Yoga Mat! No, you fool! Yoga Mat is in fact the last thing you need! Instead of sparing their loved ones from their company at least on this one day, they hang around with each other as if on a picnic! If I could, I would really have come naked to the programme, leave alone carrying a Yoga mat with me. I felt this Guru is a man of great compassion offering such priceless tools just for a few thousand bucks to idiots of all kinds. As far as the arrangements for the programme were concerned, it was like nothing I had ever experienced before. As soon as I entered the venue, smiling volunteers stood all over - gracefully welcoming the participants but to be honest, they really won me over with one seemingly small yet significant detail - the way participant's footwear were neatly organised outside the venue. I was floored. To bother doing that with over 8000 footwears for me seemed like the work of a Perfect Master.

But what really melted my apprehensions away is the aesthetics of the entire programme. Right from the way the Guru presented himself, the music being played during breaks, the live classical music performances from modestly yet gracefully dressed kids - all of this while they sat absolutely still, the decor of the entire place. If the divine ever conducted a programme, I would expect it to be like this. The entire programme seemed like a piece of art! Now, I will not divulge more details about the programme as it is against both - programme rules and my own ethics. I don't want it to be a hindrance to anybody's experience should they choose to try it someday. But what I can share is my experience of the programme, part of which I have already done. Now, I personally struggled through the programme just from my inability to sit down on the floor with folded legs beyond 3 seconds! My body became a huge hindrance, just as it did during my Vipassana. Now, somewhere during the programme, the Guru announces that there is going to be an initiation. INITIATION? I don't know how but I knew what this meant and knowing what it means, it freaked me out. An initiation, known as a Shaktipat in the Yogic parlance is a transmission of energy from the Guru to a disciple. How do I put this? So, in Yogic sciences, there is a particular set of practices called Kriya Yoga, or the Yoga of Energy. It is in many ways the most potent of all technologies, usually designed by frontbencher Yogis, for front bencher Yogis only. Because it is so potent, it is also very dangerous so the Shaktipat plays 2 key roles - one it acts like a sim card to your phone. A phone without a sim card is of some use but not usable for its core function which is to make calls. Similarly, the Yogic practise itself is only as useful as its initiation. Also, energy wise if things go haywire in the person either due to doing the practice incorrectly or for any other reason, it can ruin the person in many ways so the energy support keeps a tab of all that. Then also, how you receive the Shaktipat determines the course of your practice and consequently spiritual journey so it is most conducive to keep yourself pure and receptive during initiation. With my body being a hindrance, my mind was very disturbed and restless in the run-up to the initiation so I did something simple to fix it. There is this one song composed by the great Master Gurdjieff (known as the Rascal Saint) that would always accentuate the spiritual longing within me and almost always bring me to tears. At the time of initiation, I just played that song in my head. I shall not describe what happened precisely, but let's say I knew I received the Shaktipat from the Guru in a very beautiful way. Who is this man? I don't seem to fully understand but I hope I do someday. Two suggestions were made during the programme - both of which made me chuckle. One, they said that in order to establish the practice within the system everyone was advised to do the practice twice(roughly 40 mins each session) for at least 40 days, a significant period known as a Mandala in Yogic sciences. All of this Yoga is new to me and I told myself I will take my own sweet time to complete my mandala. I also felt, it is high time I resumed working. The second suggestion was made in response to a question someone asked - What is the best time to do the practise? 3:30 - 5:30 am came a quick response. There were chuckles all over the venue, mine included.

Now, because we are just getting started, I am going to segregate the story to you as Personal, Work, and Spiritual, but very soon what is personal, spiritual, and work will be all over the place and it all merges into one.

Work - After roughly a year of Spiritual searching, I resumed my passion project of changing the education system. My TEDx talk was still going strong, and I continued to receive countless emails extending their support and wishes to me. I started reaching out to a lot of EdTech start-ups who too set out to change the education system, but it was quite frustrating to talk to them. None of them really cared about the system. All of them only wanted to make money. For the first time, I realised capitalism is not the answer to everything, most certainly not education. Everything I stood for was being put to the test now. I had no interest in founding another EdTech start-up, although given my credibility in the field then because of my book and TEDx talk, it would have been much easier for me to do. I knew the problem of education warrants a more socialist approach. I knew my spiritual growth was also crucial before I set out to solve a problem as important as the education system. Unless I had answers, how could I design a solution?

Personally - My mother was beginning to get a little concerned. Fully aware of my propensity to go to extreme lengths, she would rather have me smoke and drink than be involved in this newfound obsession with Spirituality.

Spiritually - Before my initiation, I thought I would manage my practices the way I want to, but it turned out to be the other way round. My entire life started revolving around the schedule for both my practices. It was beyond me! It just took over my life. Much later, I read a blog from Him stating that there are some people who He calls fortunate, who He initiates in such a way that for them practices become compulsive. I saw what He was doing with me, and no matter how much gratitude you add to infinite, it still remains infinite. Strange things started happening, of which I would like to mention one particular incident. I was at a local D-Mart shopping for groceries, and suddenly one sound or mantra came to me as I stood in the line to pay for my order. It wasn't quite clear to me, but I could catch the sound and some words from it. On Googling, I realised it was Nam Myoh Ho Renge Kyo - the cornerstone mantra and the basis of the Nichiren Buddhist practice. I could only attribute this strange occurrence to my involvement with the Buddhist practice in a previous lifetime.

Another thing that happened was I received 3 back-to-back invites for talks. This never happened before, but the important thing was all these talks were either at or around spiritually significant places.

Then over a period of 2 days, I was to hit both an absolute low and absolute high in my life. The low happened just a day before Diwali when the guys from the power supply disconnected electric service to our house just a day before what is the festival of lights in India. This had happened due to non-payment of bills. Largely, God has been kind to the family. We never felt short of anything, but we were still essentially middle-class. My dad had retired, and a chunk of money was spent on his cancer treatment. There may not have been enough money to pay all the bills. I was busy with my own dreams, ambition to change the education system, and now for the last year or so Spiritual exploration. All this while, my mother didn't utter a word to me. Instead, she put the pressure of earning money on my younger sister. As an entrepreneur, it is a common experience most people go through so I won't romanticise my suffering; it is part of the thrill of building something. Personally, I didn't feel bad, but I felt really bad for my mother that she had to go through all of this for the unusual life I chose to live. I consoled myself by recollecting the story of the Great Swami Vivekananda, whose spiritual path left his family in utter poverty. In his own words *"On the one hand, I would have to see my mother and brothers starve unto death; on the other, I had believed that this man's ideas were for the good of India and the world, and had to be preached and worked out. What if a mother or 2 brothers die? It is one kind of sacrifice. Let it be done. No great thing can be done without sacrifice. The heart must be plucked out and the bleeding heart placed upon the altar. Then great things are done. I appeal to each one of you, to those who have accomplished any great thing. Oh, how much it has cost. What agony! What torture! What terrible suffering is behind every deed of success in every life"*

What is my suffering compared to His, I asked myself?

We somehow got out of that situation quickly, and the light was back in the house in time for Diwali. On the day of Diwali, something strange happened in my building. 4-5 snakes appeared out of nowhere. I didn't know of this until later in the day. I learnt from Him that snakes are extremely sensitive to certain energies and are easily drawn to places with heightened energies. Little did I know what these creatures were sensing. I would find out soon. That day, during my practice, in a moment, I knew everything there is to know. Everything. I had "The Experience." For a few moments, I had become The Truth. Who am I, Who are You, Who is God? Is life a dream, if yes whose dream are we in? What is Enlightenment? Who is a Guru? I knew everything. I became everything. There was dance. A Cosmic Dance. A smile of a very distinct kind graced my countenance. Of mischief. Of Grace. Of Divinity. Of Knowing. Of Realizing. Of Love. What did I experience? I shall not tell you. I have never shared this with anyone yet, and I don't see that changing. It's perhaps a secret I shall leave with someday. In spirituality, the role of experiences is only twofold - to either attract you to the path or keep you on it. My speculation is that I received this dramatic experience after the previous day's debacle so that I don't give up on what I set upon. So what does my experience tell me - is Spiritual Growth worth pursuing? Hell Yeah! Is Enlightenment the supposed highest goal of life worth pursuing in spite of all the vagaries it brings? Hell yeah! In fact, Heaven yeah! But the path to it could be hellish.

In Spirituality, experiences don't mean anything if they don't transform you. If you are given a tremendous experience and you go about your life as usual after it, it's pointless. In my case, "The Experience" flipped my life upside down. These were the major takeaways for me -

1- I needed to report to my boss (Him) immediately.

2- Who is a Guru? Let's say, if you could invite one person from the future to guide you in your present, who would it be? Your parents? Perhaps not because they may have their own vested interest and not necessarily always your best interest. Your friends? No. They may have your best interest but they may not know everything about your life.

There is only one person best suited for the job. You. The Future You. Who else knows everything about you and wants the best for You? Only You. So a Guru is essentially just that - a best version of yourself from the future, who knows your past, present, and future and only wants the best for you.

3- A Guru is the most successful project manager in the Universe. If he picks you as His project, He will make sure you reach your end goal. He will pull strings, do whatever, but He (and You) shall succeed. But being picked is the crucial deal.

4- K(who I mentioned previously too in the context of K &A) had now officially made an entry into my life. Unofficially, perhaps He was always there, mischievously hidden.

My immediate goal was to approach Him for a meeting. I knew what I was asking for. I also knew meeting Him requires immense Karmic fortune. I was willing to give it a shot. After meeting Him, I would want to move to his ashram for 6 months, working closely with the schools he built. This would not only help me understand what an ideal education should look like, but it would help me explore human consciousness and propel my spiritual growth. In a nutshell, what I had to do was extremely clear to me - I just wasn't ready for it yet, so sought His guidance in getting me there. I know it sounds too vague and abstract, but it is all I can say for now.

Depending on who came and asked me, I always gave different answers for what I was up to in life, but the reality was for 6 months, I did nothing but waited patiently to meet Him. Various interactions with His team were going nowhere. Would I have waited for 6 years? Yeah. Maybe even 6 lifetimes! I knew what it meant to meet an Enlightened Master. One day my Mother couldn't contain her concerns about me and the family and for the first time, urged me to take up a job. This may sound arrogant, but it's true. I knew meeting Him was my birthright. If needed, I would even bring my mom into the picture! She would create a ruckus in the ashram and somehow arrange for a meeting with Him for me. After my mother's reprimand and frustrated at the discussion with His team going nowhere, I took a screenshot of my Inbox and sent it to His team with the text "These are all the kids who write to me hoping for a change in the education system. Please let me know if a meeting with Him is possible, else I shall tell all these kids to mind their own business and I shall go and find a job too."

I still remember that day and moment vividly. It was 28th of May 2018. I sat down for my practice. As was the habit, I checked my phone first thing after it was done.

I didn't want to overwhelm myself with the enormity of what I had gotten into, so I kept myself distracted with preparation. When I say preparation, not in terms of what I was going to speak to Him. I didn't care about that. What I sought was so clear within me that I knew there would be no reason for Him to ask me nor for me to say it in words. What was it? It had nothing to do with anything you may be able to guess right now. Just in case he did ask me, I knew exactly what to say anyway. In one crisp line. So my preparation was of a different kind. It was more about how I would present myself to Him. I knew I could receive a lot from this meeting simply by being there, in the same space as Him. And in order to receive the full extent of what I can, I had planned in some detail how I would prepare over the next 3 weeks. First thing, I moved to my former house in Bangalore, where Tanush and Prashant still lived. I had informed at home that I was going to hunt for a job in Bangalore, which was partially true. I wanted to be away from home as I prepared. In peace. Plus it was also closer to the ashram where he resided. When in Bangalore, I went on a 100% raw diet. As per His own teaching, the human body consumes most energy in conducting 2 activities - ingesting and digesting. As raw food is easily digested, it conserves more energy, thereby fuelling and enabling higher states of consciousness. Those days, I could barely sit still or even straight without leaning my back, so I practised sitting with an erect posture, often leaning against the wall, all day long. Because Mou, his member of staff with whom I was co-ordinating, had asked me to prepare a presentation for my plan, I took Prashant's help in having a PPT ready. Prashant worked at McKinsey and those guys are literally paid shit loads of money to do just that - make PPTs so together, we prepared something. I didn't pay much head to the presentation because I knew I WAS THE FUCKING PLAN! No, really. Of course, I made a mental note to myself "Adhi, no matter how cool it sounds, you are never going to say that line to Mou . Actually to anyone." As I prepared, and with my next project hanging by the fate of my meeting with Him, I had to while away time, so I spent most times watching movies and for some reason, a lot of them being regional Indian or foreign language movies. I realised there is a world of quality cinema outside the mainstream Hollywood and Bollywood movies I was used to watching until then. I told myself that someday, I would love to do something to boost regional storytelling. Of course, needless to say, my practices were on twice a day as it always had been. While the meeting was scheduled for the 29th of June, I decided to get there a few days early and arrived on the 25th . If one has been initiated into any of the practices from the Guru, then you could stay in the ashram for a minimum of 3 days with prior registration and confirmation. During your stay, you shall be provided with dormitory accommodation, 2 filling meals a day and be expected to involve yourself in activity, or volunteering service during your stay. Of course, I was instructed to report for my volunteering activity. Of course, I did not. Then I received a follow-up call and I found it very strange. Whosoever the volunteer was , clearly knew that I didn't report to my activity and she was calling me so that I reported to my activity soon. I had never seen an Indian speak like that before. She called me and said, "Anna have you reported to your activity today Anna." Of course you know I haven't! Why are you asking me? What if I said Yes? I found this very strange because this is a very American way of doing things. You know Passive Aggressive? And I don't mean it in a negative way at all. It is quite admirable actually. Americans really are the Masters of PR. They know the art of saying a lot yet not saying anything really! Have you read the PR releases that American celebrities make when they are caught in a scandal? How companies respond to mass layoffs, declining revenues or anything unsavoury? It's absolutely brilliant how craftily and carefully they frame sentences. And this is a trait that the Average American has! Not just the guys on top. It's in the blood! This is far from the Indian way of dealing with things who tend to be more emotionally transparent and outspoken. Anyway, I just ignored this volunteer's call because well, it's me! But that wasn't the only reason. As soon as I arrived at the ashram, I got a panic attack. My early impression of the ashram was that I found it very overwhelming and also alarmingly strange. His photos were all over the place with people literally worshipping His photos and bowing down to them. There was also a morning ritual and an important one at that in the ashram scheme of things to perform a pooja to His photo and then start the morning practices. This was a radically new thing for me, particularly to perform it to a living person. Even by factoring into account the fateful experience I had and the consequent insight I had into an enlightened being. Also, such a ritual seemed in contrast to the teaching I had initially signed up for which revolved more around the energy and the body than a set of rituals. Another sight that intimidated me in a big way was when I saw some strange men and women wearing peculiar attires, with shaven heads and sombre looking faces. There was no doubt something very distinct, dignified and graceful about their presence which I couldn't ignore. Later, I came to know they were resident monks. So, to see all these people worship Him like a God and to realise that I will be meeting Him in person just in a few days, I panicked and I immediately messaged my cousin Shiva, an old accomplice and seasoned victim of my adventures. I told him that I don't think I am ready to meet Him and that I feel like returning back to Mumbai. Quite strangely, he said something wise which again felt like one of those moments when something else was speaking via him. My brother said, "If you weren't ready, he wouldn't have called you." Made sense so I decided to stay back. I also dropped a message to Mou saying I had arrived in the ashram and will be ready to see Him on 29th, which was 4 days away. So I had time for this mental turbulence to settle. The following morning on the 26th, I received an email response from Mou inviting me to see her. I knew exactly why she wanted to see me. After visiting the ashram, I realised how big a deal He is for the people there. They literally treat Him like God so getting to meet Him in person is actually a pretty BIG deal. I think she just wanted to see me to make sure who she was going to place in front of Him. So I met her, at the lobby of her residential quarters which is one of the more premium quarters in the ashram. I came in first and after an anxious wait of just a few minutes, she showed up. Gracefully dressed in a brown saree, with salt and pepper hair, indicating her seasoned experience both with life and work, must be in her 50s.

The first half of the meeting was, well, how do I say this, DISASTROUS? She is a woman with tremendous corporate experience, so naturally my plan (or the lack of it) didn't impress her much. To make matters worse, GUESS WHAT?! I did tell her that I AM THE PLAN. Hope you felt second-hand embarrassment from reading that. Because I felt it again after writing about it. Anyway, got to give it to the lady, she may have been shrewd in her interrogation but very patient, nonetheless. The second half of the 45 min long meeting, she literally tried to extract reasons from me instead of simply giving up. In the process, she opened my TEDx talk, viewed some of my media interviews, so with all of this, the meeting concluded with me offering her a copy of my book. She told me to keep my phone handy for the next couple of minutes, and she would confirm to me if the meeting would be possible or not. I knew this was coming. Once I came to the ashram, I knew the prospect of meeting him seemed too good to be true. I sent a text to Tanush and my brother saying that there is a 50% chance I would get to meet Him. I had come to terms with either possibility. I knew if I did enter that room to meet Him, then my life would never be the same. If I didn't, I was okay with it. My practices would continue no matter where I am, and life will move on fine. So I was okay with both or at least pretending to be so.

It seems in the afternoon they serve juice in the community dining hall. So what if I didn't contribute to any volunteering activity to earn it, but oh boy, just for that interrogation, I definitely deserve the juice, okay? 😊 I get there, I start talking to a random guy having juice, and just then a friend known to him comes visibly animated and tearful.

On enquiring why he was so, it turns out that on his way to the hall, he encountered Him on the bike, and He greeted this boy as He passed by - a moment so overwhelming for him that he couldn't contain his tears. In my head, I still think, what have I signed up for? And just then, at that very moment, I get a text message from Mou - "Get ready, you are meeting him in the next 45 mins." Meeting Him in the next 45 mins? MEETING HIM IN THE NEXT 45 MINS? WHAT DO YOU MEAN?! PLEASE TELL ME THIS IS A PRANK. I am hoping a television crew will show up with all the secret cameras and tell me this is a prank. I kid you not, all the juices in my body went dry, and a sense of numbness that I had never experienced before engulfed me. I was supposed to meet him 3 days later and still haven't come to terms with it. What on Earth could prepare me to meet him in the next 45 mins? I HAVE A MEETING. WITH GOD. IN 45 freaking minutes! WTF!

You may perhaps wonder, and understandably so, why such an over the top reaction to meeting anyone? Now let's say, you take an Amazonian tribesman to meet Cristiano Ronaldo, the meet may mean nothing to him and Ronaldo may appear like just another human to the tribesman. However, if you take any football fan to meet Ronaldo, for them, the guy is no less than God. Given his God-like mastery and accomplishments over the game, Ronaldo holds a significance much more than of an ordinary human being. Similarly, given "The Experience" and knowing who this Guru is - or any Guru is - beyond the distraction of persona, I knew fully the significance of meeting an Enlightened Being. I was literally going to meet God! Why do I say so? We shall look at who or rather what God/Godliness is in great detail in Volume 2.

Now, I knew He was a man of great taste and aesthetics. I also knew the significance of wearing white when in divine presence, so keeping both of that in mind, I had brought with me a fully washed and neatly ironed pair of pristine white shirt and a Veshti, which is an unstitched cloth elegantly draped around the lower body, an attire traditional to South Indian men. However, I was nowhere within the vicinity of sanity to have the sense or balance to go to my dorm, change my clothes, and then be in time for the meeting, so I simply decided to see him in what I was wearing at the time of meeting Mou - a Navy Blue shirt and Denims at the bottom. "For a Master, the body itself is an attire, so why would he care about what I wear anyway?" I said to myself in justification of my own decision. Mou and I meet at a pre-decided assembly point from where she takes me with her to His office. On our way, she tells me, "I read a bit of your book and it looks like you have God's Grace," kind words that did little to shake off my anxiety that was reaching heights so towering that it could put the mountain ranges that surrounded me to shame. But I think she made the decision to let me meet Him after reading my book, for which I am so very thankful. The restless energy within me wants to find expression in violent ways - I want to run, shake myself, or jump, but then I have to keep pace with Mou , so I do none of these. She escorts me to one of his 2 offices. This one has a wide wooden gate, about 4 - 5 feet tall and 15 feet wide at the Main Entrance. Outside the gate is a small waiting area, a shelter under which is a wide rectangular piece of rock that can accommodate around 5-6 people. What aesthetics this place has! Even the most insignificant things look like a piece of art. I wait along with 3 of His monks who I assume are there to see Him after me. Now fully unapologetic and unable to contain my nervousness, I stop caring about outside perception, so every few seconds, I get up, walk around nervously, sit down, and repeat. In cycles of 5 seconds. Incessantly.

Tbh, I have lost it! I knew when this day would come, I would be walking into my death. What does that mean? I don't know. Mou notices my mannerisms and prescribes to me a particular breathing technique, which I later realise is this place's panacea for everything. You know, Indian parents and most certainly my mom, when I was growing up, prescribed a haircut for any problem I went to her with. Headache? Because of long hair. Insomnia? Again, because of my long hair. Israel-Palestine conflict? Obviously because of my long hair. Similarly, here also this breathing technique is like that. Any problem, they prescribe you this 😄

Not wanting to disrespect her, I pretended to do it for a few seconds, then went back to my nervous routine. "Can you suggest some Do's and Don'ts on how to be with him?" I ask her diffidently. "Umm, if he doesn't seem impressed, just change the topic," came her clear response, which my mind made a note of (or did it? DID YOU, MIND? DID YOU? ARE YOU EVEN LISTENING?)

There is one line from my book, which I have tried and tested countless times, and it has had a spotless track record of getting the listener's attention. The line goes like this - "If engineering were a religion, it would be the fifth biggest religion in India." It's almost like a spell after which I tell them more about the book and anything else I want to discuss. This is literally the only preparation as far as the conversation aspect of it is concerned. Mou gestures to me to follow her. Fuck, fuck, fuck. We are now entering the main gate where his security in-charge directs me to keep my phone on silent. SILENT? YOU CAN KEEP THE GOD-DAMN PHONE, KIND SIR! I just thrust my phone upon him and walked inside. Equipped with the knowledge of who a Guru really is, there was no need or desire in me to click a photo with him. iPad is mostly for note-taking. Book so that I can offer him a copy. Not for him to read, of course. Just as an offering! What a fortune to be able to present the Universal Consciousness with a piece of my work? Mou and I wait outside His cabin inside which He is seated, and we are joined by another member from his office on whose green signal we are supposed to enter inside. My body and mind are both overwhelmed beyond capacity. I just cannot take this tension anymore. It felt like at least 58,000 years had passed by since the time Mou sent me that text after our meeting and to this point waiting outside His cabin. My heart is pounding like a concert; with every inhalation, my mental ambience is tenser. I want to just run away from all of this. I don't know why I got into this in the first place. Amma, please help me.

We receive a green signal to enter the room. Mou insists I open the door. I take a deep breath before entering and then open the door. Yes, I walked into my own death......

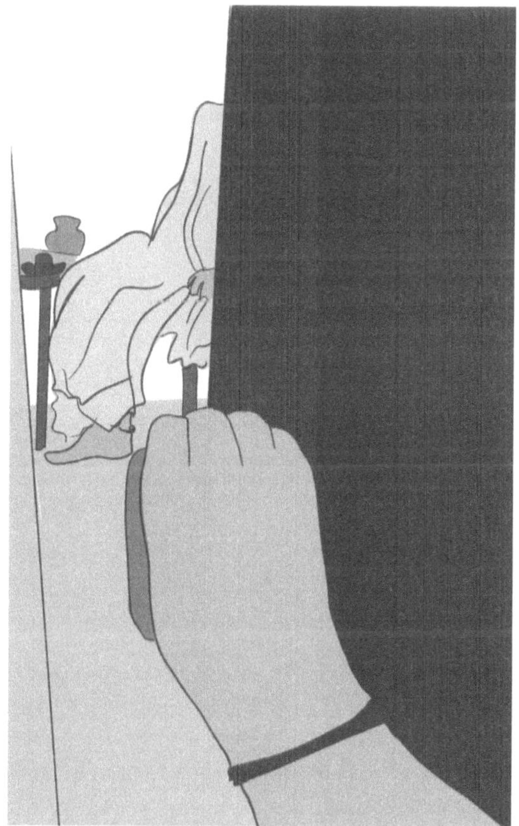

Please scan this code to unlock $GIC tokens and
Bonus content for this chapter

To follow Lekha on Instagram, scan the QR code below

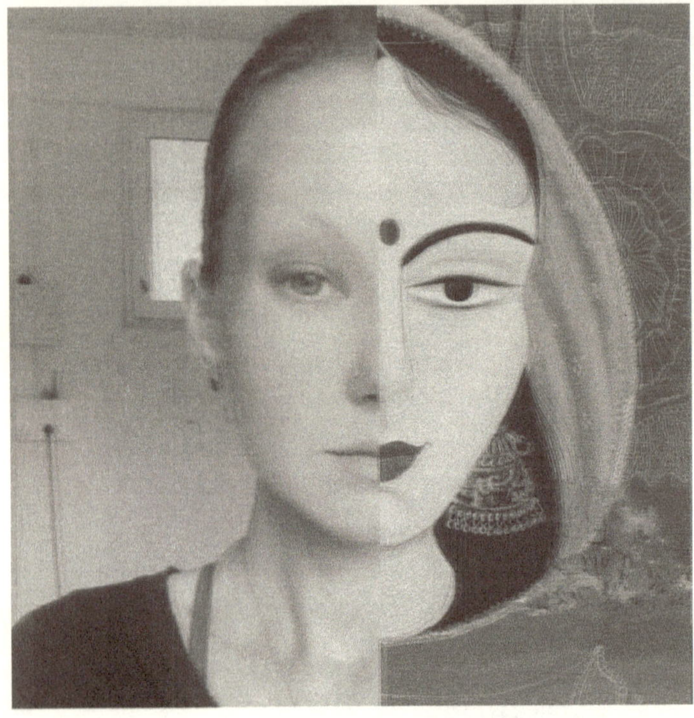

To follow Katia Ram on Instagram, scan the QR code below

I prefer the classic form of conversation - Letters/Hand-written notes. Scan the QR code below for the postal address.

Alternatively, you can send me an email - adhi316@gmail.com

I give you this (embarrassing) childhood email -id that I only share for personal communication.

Question 7 -

Who Are You?

Question 7 -

Who Are You?